STORIES IN VERSE.

STORIES IN VERSE.

BY

HENRY ABBEY.

The sense of the world is short —
To love and be beloved.

EMERSON.

NEW YORK:
A. D. F. RANDOLPH & CO., PUBLISHERS,
COR. BROADWAY AND NINTH STREET.
1869.

RIVERSIDE, CAMBRIDGE:
PRINTED BY H. O. HOUGHTON AND COMPANY.

TO

RICHARD GRANT WHITE,

WITH GRATITUDE FOR HIS FRIENDSHIP, AND WITH ADMIRATION
FOR HIS ELEGANT SCHOLARSHIP.

CONTENTS.

BLANCHE:

AN EXHALATION FROM WITHERED VIOLETS.

I.

THE VENDER OF VIOLETS.

"VIOLETS! Violets! Violets!"
This was the cry I heard
As I passed through the street of a city;
And quickly my heart was stirred
To an incomprehensible pity,
At the undertone of the cry;
For it seemed like the voice of one
Who was stricken, and all undone,
Who was only longing to die.

"Violets! Violets! Violets!"
The voice came nearer still.
"Surely," I said, "it is May,
And out on valley and hill,
The violets blooming to-day,
Send this invitation to me
To come and be with them once more;

I know they are dear as can be,
And I hate the town with its roar.

"Violets! Violets! Violets!"
Children of sun and of dew,
Flakes of the blue of the sky,
There is somebody calling to you
Who seems to be longing to die;
Yet violets are so sweet
They can scarcely have dealings with death.
Can it be, that the dying breath,
That comes from the one last beat
Of a true heart, turns to the flowers?

"Violets! Violets! Violets!"
The crier is near me at last.
With my eyes I am holding her fast.
She is a lovely seller of flowers.
She is one whom the town devours
In its jaws of bustle and strife.
How poverty grinds down a life;
For, lost in the slime of a city,
What is a beautiful face?
Few are they who have pity
For loveliness in disgrace.
Yet she that I hold with my eyes,
Who seems so modest and wise,
Has not yet fallen, I am sure.
She has nobly learned to endure.
Large, and mournful, and meek,

Her eyes seem to drink from my own.
Her curls are carelessly thrown
Back from white shoulder and cheek;
And her lips seem strawberries, lost
In some Arctic country of frost.
The slightest curve on a face,
May give an expression unmeet;
Yet hers is so perfect and sweet,
And shaped with such delicate grace,
Its loveliness is complete.

"Violets! Violets! Violets!"
I hear the cry once more;
But not as I heard it before.
It whispers no more of death;
But only of odorous breath,
And modest flowers, and life.
I purchased a cluster, so rife
With the touch of her tapering hand,
I seem to hold it in mine.
I would I could understand,
Why a touch seems so divine.

II.

A FLOWER FOUND IN THE STREET.

To-day in passing down the street,
  I found a flower upon the walk,
A dear syringa, white and sweet,
  Wrung idly from the missing stalk.

And something in its odor speaks
  Of dark brown eyes, and arms of snow,
And rainbow smiles on sunset cheeks —
  The maid I saw a month ago.

I waited for her many a day,
  On the dear ground where first we met;
I sought her up and down the way,
  And all in vain I seek her yet.

Syringa, naught your odor tells,
  Or whispers so I cannot hear;
Speak out, and tell me where she dwells,
  In perfume accents, loud and clear.

Shake out the music of your speech,
  In quavers of delicious breath;
The conscious melody may teach
  A lover where love wandereth.

If so you speak, with smile and look,
  You will not wither, but endure;
And in my heart's still open book,
  Keep your white petals ever pure.

If so you speak, upon her breast
  You yet may rest, nor sigh afar;
But in the moonlight's silver dressed,
  Seem 'gainst your heaven the evening star.

III.

ODYLE.

We know that they are often near
Of whom we think, of whom we talk,
Though we have missed them many a year,
And lost them from our daily walk.

Some strange clairvoyance dwells in all,
And webs the souls of human kind.
I would that I could learn its thrall,
And know the power of mind on mind.

I then might quickly use the sense,
To find where one I worship dwells,
If in the city, or if thence
Among the breeze-rung lily bells.

IV.

WHAT ONE FINDS IN THE COUNTRY.

I went out in the country
To spend an idle day —
To see the flowers in blossom,
And scent the fragrant hay.

The dawn's spears smote the mountains
Upon their shields of blue,
And space, in her black valleys,
Joined in the conflict too.

The clouds were jellied amber;
  The crickets in the grass
Blew pipe and hammered tabor,
  And laughed to see me pass.

The cows down in the pasture,
  The mowers in the field,
The birds that sang in heaven,
  Their happiness revealed.

My heart was light and joyful,
  I could not answer why;
And I thought that it was better
  Always to smile than sigh.

How could I hope to meet her
  Whom most I wished to meet?
If always I had lost her,
  Then life were incomplete.

The road ran o'er a brooklet;
  Upon the bridge she stood,
With wild flowers in her ringlets,
  And in her hand her hood.

The morn laid on her features
  An envious golden kiss;
She might have fancied truly,
  I longed to share its bliss.

I said, "O, lovely maiden,
  I have sought you many a day.
That I love you, love you, love you,
  Is all that I can say."

Her mournful eyes grew brighter,
  And archly glanced, though meek.
A bacchanalian dimple
  Dipt a wine-cup in her cheek.

"If you love me, love me, love me,
  If you love me as you say,
You must prove it, prove it, prove it!"
  And she lightly turned away.

V.

AN AUNT AND AN UNCLE.

I have but an aunt and an uncle
  For kinsfolk on the earth,
And one has passed me unnoticed
  And hated me from my birth;
But the first has reared me and taught me,
  Whatever I have of worth.

This is my uncle by marriage,
  For his wife my aunt had died,
And left him all her possessions,
  With much that was mine beside —

'Tis said that he hated her brother,
As much as he loved the bride.

That brother, my father, forgave him,
As his last hour ran its sand,
And begged in return his forgiveness,
As he placed in his sister's hand
The bonds, that when I was twenty,
Should be at my command.

For my mother was dead, God rest her,
And I would be left alone.
The bride to her trust was unfaithful —
Her heart was harder than stone.
And her widowed sister, left childless,
Adopted me as her own.

So we dwelt in opposite houses —
We in a dwelling low,
And he in a brown stone mansion.
I toiled and my gain was slow.
My uncle rode in a carriage
As fine as there was in the row.

Once, in a useless anger,
With courage not mine before,
I bearded the crafty lion,
Demanding my own, no more.
He said the law gave me nothing,
And showed me out of his door.

VI.

MY AUNT INVITES HER IN TO DINE.

This is the place, this is the hour,
And through the shine, or through the shower,
  She promised she would come.
O, darling day, she is so sweet
I could kneel down and kiss her feet.
  Her presence makes me dumb.

A thousand things that I would say,
And ponder when she is away,
  Desert me when she's near —
When she is near — twice we have met!
Though but a month has passed as yet,
  It seems almost a year.

O, now she comes, and here she stands,
And gives me hers in both my hands,
  And blushes to her brow.
She eyes askance her simple gown,
And folds a Judas tatter down
  She has not seen till now.

I said, "My love you made me wait,
I grew almost disconsolate
  Thinking you would not come.
Ah, tell me what you have to do,
That makes your duty, sweet, for you
  My rival in your home."

"My home!" she answered, "I have none.
For me, 'tis years since there was one,
And that was scarcely mine.
Father and mother both are dead;
I sell sweet flowers to earn my bread —
Their fragrance is my wine.

"Sometimes the house upon the farm,
Sometimes the city's friendly arm,
Shields me from rain and dew.
I did not know that it was late;
The minutes you have had to wait,
Are truly but a few."

A smile shone through her large dark eyes,
As sometimes, in the stormy skies,
The light puts through an arm,
Which, spreading glory far and wide,
Draws the broad curtain cloud aside,
Making the whole earth warm.

She took my arm; we walked away;
We saw, in parks, the fountains play;
My heart was all elate.
I scarcely noticed when I stood,
With my dear waif of womanhood,
Beside our lowly gate.

"You have no home," I gently said,
"But, till the day that we are wed,
And after if you will,

This home, my love, is mine and thine."
My aunt came out and bade us dine—
  I see her smiling still.

My Blanche, reluctant, gave consent;
Then 'neath the humble roof we went,
  And sat about the board.
I saw how sweet the whole surprise;
I saw her fond uplifted eyes,
  Give thanks unto the Lord.

VII.

THE PROPHECY.

There is a prophecy of our line,
Told by some great grand-dame of mine
I once attempted to divine.

'Tis that two children, then unborn,
Would know a wealthy wedding morn,
Or die in poverty forlorn.

These children would be of her name.
If to the bridal bans they came,
The house would gather strength and fame.

But if they came not, woe is me,
The line would ever cease to be,
The wealth would take its wings and flee.

If all the signs are coming true,
I am the child she pictured, who
The name should keep or hide from view.

In our domain of liberty,
Our heed is light of pedigree,
I care not for the prophecy.

For what to me our wealth or line?
I only wish to make her mine —
The maid my aunt asked in to dine.

VIII.

HOW A POOR GIRL WAS MADE RICH.

All the day my toil was easy, for I knew that in the evening,
I could go home from my labor, and find Blanche at the door;
How could I dream the sunlight in my sky was so deceiving?
And I ceased in my believing 'twould be cloudy ever more.

When at last the twilight deepened, I entered our low dwelling,
And my darling rose to meet me, with the love-light in her eyes;
On that day her simple story to my aunt she had been telling,

And I saw her words were welling, fraught with ominous surprise.

For it seems my hated uncle, once had given him a daughter,
Who on a saddened morning had been stolen from the door,
And through the panting city the criers cried and sought her,
But in vain; they never brought her to his threshold any more.

Blanche was she, my uncle's daughter; no unwelcome truth was plainer;
For a small peculiar birth-mark was apparent on her arm.
Had I lost her? Was it possible ever more now to regain her?
Would he spurn me, and restrain her with his wily golden charm?

All that night my heart was bitter with unutterable anguish,
And I cried out in my slumber till with my words I woke:
"How long, O Lord, must poverty bow down its head and languish,
While wrong, with wealth to garnish it, makes strong the heavy yoke?"

IX.

THE MISER.

'Tis said, that when he saw his child,
  And saw the proof that she was his,
The first in many a year he smiled,
  And pressed upon her brow a kiss.

In both his hands her hand he bound,
  And led her gayly through his place.
He said the dead years circled round,
  Hers was so like her mother's face.

He scarcely moves him from her side —
  Her every hour with joy beguiles.
To make the gulf between us wide,
  He acts the miser of her smiles.

He brings her presents rich and rare —
  Wrought gold by cunning hands impearled,
Round opals that with scarlet glare,
  The lightning of each mimic world.

X.

SHE PASSED ME BY.

She bowed, and smiled, and passed me by,
    She passed me by!
O love, O lava breath that burns,
'Tis hard indeed to think she spurns
  Such worshippers as you and I.

She smiled, and bowed, with stately pride;
The bow the frosty smile belied.
  She passed me by.

She bowed, and smiled, and passed me by,
  She passed me by.
What more could any maiden do?
It did not prove she was untrue.
 My heart is tired, I know not why.
I only know I weep and pray.
Love has its night as well as day.
  She passed me by.

XI.

MIND WITHOUT SOUL.

Some strange story I have read
  Of a man without a soul.
Mind he had, though soul had fled;
Magic gave him gifts instead,
  And the form of youth he stole.

Grows a rose-azalea white,
  In my garden, near the way.
I who see it with delight,
Dream its soul of odor might,
  In the past, have fled away.

Blanche (O, sweet, you are so fair,
  So sweet, so fair, whate'er you do),

Twine no azalea in your hair,
Lest I think in my despair,
Heart and soul have left you too.

XII.

A BROKEN SWORD.

Deep in the night I saw the sea,
And overhead, the round moon white;
Its steel cold gleam lay on the lea,
And seemed my sword of life and light,
Broke in that war death waged with me.

I heard the dip of golden oars;
Twelve angels stranded in a boat;
We sailed away for other shores;
Though but an hour we were afloat,
We harbored under heavenly doors.

O, Blanche, if I had run my race,
And if I wore my winding sheet,
And mourners went about the place,
Would you so much as cross the street,
To kiss in death my white, cold face?

XIII.

A CHANCE FOR GAIN.

I met him in the busy mart;
His eyes are large, his lips are firm,
And on his temples, care or sin

Has left its claw prints hardened in;
His step is nervous and infirm;
I wondered if he had a heart.

He blandly smiled and took my hand.
He owed me such a debt, he thought,
He felt he never could repay;
Yet should I call on him that day,
He'd hand me what the papers brought,
For which I once had made demand.

Then added, turning grave from gay;
"But you must promise, if I give,
Your lover's office to resign,
And stand no more 'twixt me and mine."
His words were water in a sieve.
I turned my back and strode away.

XIV.

THE LIGHT-HOUSE.

At twilight, past the fountain,
I wandered in the park,
And saw a closed white lily
Sway on the liquid dark;
And a fire-fly, perched upon it,
Shone out its fitful spark.

I fancied it a light-house
Mooned on a sky-like sea,

To warn the fearless sailors
  Of lurking treachery —
Of unseen reefs and shallows
  That starved for wrecks to be.

O Blanche, O love that spurns me,
  'Tis but a cheat thou art.
I would some friendly light-house
  Had warned me to depart
From the secret reefs and shallows
  That hide about your heart.

XV.

DARKNESS.

My hopes and my ambition all were down,
  Like grass the mower turneth from its place;
The night's thick darkness was an angry frown,
  And earth a tear upon the cheek of space.

The mighty fiend of storm in wild unrest,
  By lightning stabbed, dragged slowly up the plain;
Great clots of light, like blood, dripped down his breast,
  And from his open jaws fell foam in rain.

XVI.

IN THE CHURCH-YARD.

Where the sun shineth,
  Through the willow trees,

And the church standeth,
'Mid the tomb-stones white,
Planting anemones
I saw my delight.

Her mother sleepeth
Beneath the green mound;
A white cross standeth
To show man the place.
Now close to the ground
Blanche bendeth her face.

She quickly riseth
As she hears my walk,
And sadly smileth
Through mists of tears;
We mournfully talk
Of departed years.

She downward droopeth
Her beautiful head,
And a blue-bell seemeth
That blossometh down;
Trembling with dread,
Lest the sky should frown.

She dearer seemeth
Than ever before.
She gently chideth

My more distant way.
At her heart's one door
I entered to-day.

No palace standeth
As happy as this.
Love ever ruleth
Its precincts alone —
His sceptre a kiss,
And a smile his throne.

There is one Blanche feareth —
She loves not deceit —
She only wisheth
To dazzle his heart.
We promise to meet,
And separate depart.

XVII.

COMPARISONS.

The moon is like a shepherd with a flock of starry lambkins,
The wind is like a whisper to the mountains from the sea,
The sun a gold moth browsing on a flower's pearl-dusted pollen;
But my words can scarcely utter what my love is like to me.

She is the sun in light's magnificence across my heart's day shining,
She's the moon when through the heavens of my heart flash meteor dreams ;
Her voice is fragrant south wind a silvery sentence blowing ;
She is sweeter than the sweetest, she is better than she seems.

XVIII.

AN INQUIRY OF THE SEXTON.

"Sexton, was she here to-day
  Who has met me oft before?
Did she come and go away,
  Tired of waiting any more?
For I fancy some mistake
  Has occurred about the time;
Yet, the hour has not yet passed;
  Hark! the bells begin to chime.

"In her hair two roses woo,
  One a white, and one a red.
Azure silk her dress might be,
  Though she oft wears white instead.
Here, beside this marble cross,
  Oft she kneels in silent prayer;
Tell me, has she been to-day,
  In the church-yard anywhere?"

"No, the lady that you seek
  Has not passed the gate to-day:
I've been digging at a grave,
  And if she had come this way
I'd have seen her from my work.
  She may come to meet you yet.
I remember well her looks.
  Names, not faces, I forget."

XIX.

A RIVAL.

It seems I have a rival
  Domiciled over the way;
But Blanche, dear heart, dislikes him,
  Whatever her father may say —
This gorgeously broadclothed fellow,
  Good enough in his way.

To-day as I left the church-yard,
  I met them taking a ride,
And my heart was pierced like a buckler
  With a javelin of pride;
I only saw in my anger
  They were sitting side by side.

To-night, in the purple twilight,
  Blanche waited upon the walk,
And beckoned her white hand to me —

A lily swayed on its stalk.
Soon my jealous pride was foundered
In the maelstrom of talk.

'Twas useless to go to the church-yard,
For some one had played the spy;
She fancied it was the sexton —
We would let it all go by;
We now would have bolder meetings,
'Neath her father's very eye.

She took my arm as we idled,
And talked of our love once more,
And how, with her basket of flowers,
She had passed the street before;
We tarried long in the moonlight,
And kissed good-night at her door.

XX.

KISSES AND A RING.

I never behold the sea
Rush up to the hand of the shore,
And with its vehement lips
Kiss its down-dropt whiteness o'er,
But I think of that magic night,
When my lips, like waves on a coast,
Broke over the moonlit hand
Of her that I love the most.

I never behold the surf
  Lit by the sun into gold,
Curl and glitter and gleam,
  In a ring-like billow rolled,
But I think of another ring,
  A simple, delicate band,
That in the night of our troth
  I placed on a darling hand.

XXI.

AN ENEMY MAY BE SERVED, EVEN THROUGH MISTAKE, WITH PROFIT.

I was walking down the sidewalk,
  When up, with flying mane,
Two iron-black steeds came spurning
  The ground in wild disdain;
I caught them in an instant,
  And held them by the rein.

It seems the man had fainted
  In his elegant coupé;
I saw his face a moment,
  And then I turned away,
Wishing my steps had led me
  Through other streets that day.

Some one who saw the rescue
  Afterward told him my name.
For the first in many a season,

Beneath our roof he came.
I said I was deserving
Little of praise or blame.

It was my uncle's face in the carriage;
He made regret of the past;
No more of my love or wishes
Would he be the iconoclast;
On a gala night at his mansion
We should learn to be friends at last.

XXII.

HELIOTROPE.

Let my soul and thine commune,
Heliotrope.
O'er the way I hear the swoon
Of the music; and the moon,
Like a moth above a bloom,
Shines upon the world below.
In God's hand the world we know,
Is but as a flower in mine.
Let me see thy heart divine
Heliotrope.

Thy rare odor is thy soul,
Heliotrope.
Could I save the golden bowl,
And yet change my soul to yours,

I would do so for a day,
Just to hear my neighbors say:
"Lo! the spirit he immures
Is as fragrant as a flower;
It will wither in an hour;
Surely he has stol'n the bliss,
For we know the odor is
Heliotrope."

Have you love and have you fear,
Heliotrope?
Has a dew-drop been thy tear?
Has the south-wind been thy sigh?
Let thy soul make mine reply,
By some sense, on brain or hand,
Let me know and understand,
Heliotrope.

In thy native land, Peru,
Heliotrope,
There are worshippers of light —
They might better worship you;
But they worship not as I.
You must tell her what I say,
When I take you 'cross the way,
For to-night your petals prove
The Devotion of my love,
Heliotrope.

'Tis time we go, breath o' bee,
Heliotrope.

All the house is lit for me;
Here's the room where we may dwell,
Filled with guests delectable.
Hark! I hear the silver bell
Ever tinkling at her throat.
I have thought it was a boat,
By the Graces put afloat,
On the billows of her heart.
I have thought it was a boat
With a bird in it, whose part
Was a solitary note.
Now I know 'tis Heliotrope
That the moonlight, bursting ope,
Changed to silver on her throat.
Let us watch the dancers go;
She is dancing in the row.
Sweetest flower that ever was,
I shall give you as I pass,
Heliotrope.

KARAGWE, AN AFRICAN.

PART FIRST.

This is his story as I gathered it;
The simple story of a plain, true man.
I cling with Abraham Lincoln to the fact,
That they who make a nation truly great
Are plain men, scattered in each walk of life.
To them, my words. And if I cut, perchance,
Against the rind of prejudice, and disclose
The fruit of truth, it is for the love of truth;
And truth, I hold with Joubert, to consist
In seeing things and persons as God sees.

I.

An African, thick lipped, and heavy heeled,
With woolly hair, large eyes, and even teeth,
A forehead high, and beetling at the brows
Enough to show a strong perceptive thought
Ran out beyond the eyesight in all things —
A negro with no claim to any right,
A savage with no knowledge we possess

Of science, art, or books, or government —
Slave from a slaver to the Georgia coast,
His life disposed of at the market rate;
Yet in the face of all, a plain, true man —
Lowly and ignorant, yet brave and good,
Karagwe, named for his native tribe.

His buyer was the planter, Dalton Earl,
Of Valley Earl, an owner of broad lands,
Whose wife, in some gray daybreak of the past,
Had tarried with the night, and passed away;
But left him, as the marriage ring of death
Was slipped upon her finger, a fair child.
He called this daughter Coralline. To him
She was a spray of whitest coral, found
Upon the coast where death's impatient sea
Hems in the narrow continent of life.

II.

Each day brought health and strength to Karagwe.
Each day he worked upon the cotton-field,
And every boll he picked had thought in it.
He labored, but his mind was otherwhere;
Strange fancies, faced with ignorance and doubt,
Came peering in, each jostling each aside,
Like men, who in a crowded market-place,
Push 'gainst the mob, to see some pageant pass.

All things were new and wonderful to him.
What were the papers that his owner read?

The marks and characters, what could they mean?
If speech, what then the use of oral speech?
At last by digging round the spreading roots
Of this one thought, he found the treasure out —
Knowledge: this was the burden which was borne
By these black, busy, ant-like characters.

But how acquire the meaning of the signs?
He found a scrap of paper in the lane,
And put it by, and saved it carefully,
Till once, when all alone, he drew it forth,
And gazed at it, and strove to learn its sense.
But while he studied, Dalton Earl rode by,
And angered at the indication shown,
Snatched rudely at the paper in his hand,
And tore it up, commanding that the slave
Have fifty lashes for this breach of law.

Long on his sentence pondered Karagwe.
Against the law? Who then could make a law
Decreeing knowledge to a certain few,
To others ignorance? Surely not God;
For God, the white-haired negro with a text
Had said loved justice, and was friend to all.
If man, then the authority was null.

The fifty lashes scourged the slave's bare back,
The red blood running down at every stroke,
The dark skin clinging ghastly to the lash.
No moan escaped him at the stinging pain.

Tremblingly he stood, and patiently bore all ;
His heart indignant, shaking his broad breast,
Strong as the heart that Hippodamia wept,
Which with the cold, intrusive brass thrust through,
Shook even the Greek spear's extremity.

III.

And so the negro's energy, made strong
By the one vile argument of the lash,
Was given to learn the secret of the books.
He studied in the woods, and by the fall
Which shoots down like an arrow from the cliff,
Feathered with spray and barbed with hues of flint.
His books were bits of paper printed on,
Found here and there, brought thither by the wind.
Once standing near the bottom of the fall
And gazing up, he saw upon the verge
Of the dark cliff above him, gathering flowers,
His master's child, sweet Coralline ; she leaned
Out over the blank abyss, and smiled.
He climbed the bank, but ere he reached the height,
A shriek rang out above the water's roar ;
The babe had fallen, and a quadroon girl
Lay fainting near, upon the treacherous sward.
The babe had fallen, but with no injury yet.
Karagwe slipped down upon a narrow ledge,
And reaching out, caught hold the little frock,
Whose folds were tangled in a bending shrub,

And safely drew the child back to the cliff.
The slave had favors shown him after this,
Although he spoke not of the perilous deed,
Nor spoke of any merit he had done.

IV.

By being always when he could alone,
By wandering often in the woods and fields,
He came at last to live in revery.
But little thought is there in revery,
But little thought, for most is useless dream;
And whoso dreams may never learn to act.
The dreamer and the thinker are not kin.
Sweet revery is like a little boat
That idly drifts along a listless stream —
A painted boat, afloat without an oar.

And nature brought strange meanings to the slave;
He loved the breeze, and when he heard it pass
The agitated pines, he fancied it
The silken court-dress of the lady Wind,
Rustling among the foliage, as she went
To waltz the whirlwind on the distant sea.

The negro preacher with the text had said
That when men died, the soul lived on and on;
If so, of what material was the soul?
The eye could not behold it; why not then

The viewless air be filled with living souls?
Not only these, but other shapes and forms
Might dwell unseen about us at all times.
If air was only matter rarefied,
Why could not things still more impalpable
Have real existence? Whence came our thoughts?
As angels came to shepherds in Chaldee;
They were not ours. He fancied that most thoughts
Were whispered to the soul, or good, or bad.
The bad were like a demon, a vast shape
With measureless black wings, that when it dared,
Placed its clawed foot upon the necks of men,
And with the very shadow of itself,
Made their lives darker than a starless night.
He did not strive to picture out the good,
Or give to them a figure; but he knew
No glory of the sunset could compare
With the clear splendor of one noble deed.

He proudly dreamed that to no other mind
Had these imaginings been uttered.
Alas! poor heart, how many have awoke,
And found their newest thoughts as old as time —
Their brightest fancies woven in the threads
Of ancient poems, history or romance,
And knowledge still elusive and far off.

V.

The days that lengthen into years went on.
The quadroon girl who fainted on the cliff
Was Ruth ; now, blooming into womanhood,
She looked on Karagwe, and seeing there
Something above the level of the slave,
Watched him with interest in all his ways.

At first through pity was she drawn to him.
While both were sitting on a rustic seat,
Near the tall mansion where the planter dwelt,
A drunken overseer came straggling past,
And seeing in the dusk a female form,
Swayed up to her, and caught her by the arm,
And with an insult, strove to drag her on.
Ruth spoke not; but the negro, with one grasp
Upon the white man, caused her quick release.
He turned, and in the face struck Karagwe.
The patient slave did not return the blow,
But the next day they tied him to a post,
And fifty stripes his naked shoulders flayed.
Stricken in mind at being deeply wronged,
Filled with a noble scorn, that men most learned
Would so degrade a brother race of men,
He wept at heart; no groan fled through his lips.

Yet in a few days he was forced to go
And work beneath the intolerable sun,
Picking the cotton-boll, and bearing it

In a rude basket, on his wounded back,
Up a steep hill-side to the cotton gin.

VI.

Ruth, as she walked the pebbled garden lanes,
Or daily in her hundred household cares,
Thought of the dark face and noble heart
Of Karagwe, and truly pitied him.

He, when the labor of the day was done,
Moved through the dusk, among the dewy leaves,
And, darker than the shadows, scaled the wall,
And waited in the garden, crouching down
Among the foliage of the fragrant trees,
Hoping that she again might come that way.
He saw her through the window of the house,
Pass and repass, and heard her sweetly sing
A tender song of love and pity blent;
But would not call to her, nor give a sign
That he was there; to see her was enough.
Perhaps, if those about her knew he came
To meet her in the garden, they would place
Some punishment upon her, some restraint,
That she, though innocent, might have to bear.
So he passed back again to his low cot,
And on his poor straw pallet, dreamed of her,
As loyally perhaps as Chastelard,
Lying asleep upon his palace couch,
Dreamed of Queen Mary, and the love he gave.

VII.

Ruth was but tinged with shade, and always seemed
Some luscious fruit, with but the slightest hint
Of something foreign to the grafted bough
Whereon it grew. Her eyes were black, and large,
And passionate, and proved the deathless soul,
That through their portals looked upon the world,
Was capable of hatred and revenge.
Her long black lashes hung above their depths,
Like lotus leaves o'er some Egyptian spring.
And they were dreamy, too, at intervals,
And glowed with tender beauty when she loved.
Her grace made for her such appropriate wear,
That, though her gown was of the coarsest cloth,
And though her duty was the lowest kind,
It seemed apparel more desirable
Than trailing robes of velvet or of silk.
Her voice was full, and sweet, and musical,
Soft as the low breathings of an instrument
Touched by the unseen fingers of the breeze.

VIII.

The large plantation, next to Dalton Earl's,
Was owned by Richard Wain, a hated man —
Hated among his slaves and in the town.
Uncouth, revengeful, and a drunkard he.
Two miles up by the river ran his lands;
And here, within a green-roofed kirk of woods,

The slave found that seclusion he desired.
His only treasure was a Testament
Hid in the friendly opening of a tree.
Often the book was kept within his cot,
At times lay next his heart, nor did its beat
Defile the fruity knowledge on the leaves.
The words were sweet as wine of Eshcol grapes
To his parched lips. He saw the past arise.
Vague were the people, and the pageant moved,
Uncertain as the figures in the dusk;
Yet One there was, who stood in bold relief;
A lovely, noble face with sweeping beard,
And hair that trailed in beauty round his neck;
A patient man, whose deeds were always good,
Whose words were brave for freedom and mankind.

IX.

In passing through the grounds of Richard Wain,
Karagwe found, upon a plat of grass,
Some sheets of paper fastened at the ends,
Blown from the house, he thought, or thrown away.
The sheets were closely written on and sealed.
Here was a long-sought opportunity
To learn the older letters of the pen.
That night the writings, wrapped about the Book,
Were safe within the hollow of the tree.

X.

All day he dreamed, "What token shall I give,
That she will know my thought and understand."
He caught at last a velvet honey-bee,
Weighed down with its gold treasure in its belt,
And killed it; then, when morning came again,
Bore it to Ruth beneath the fragrant trees.
"I bring you, Ruth, a dead bee for a sign.
For if to-day you wear it in your hair,
When once again you come to walk the lane,
I then shall know that you are truly mine,
Willing to be my wife, and share my lot,
And let me toil with you like any bee;
But if you do not wear it, then I shall care
No more for anything; but waste my life,
A bee without a queen." Then not one word
Spoke Ruth; but when the sunset came, and she
Went from the house again to walk alone,
The dead bee glittered gem-like in her hair.
And him she met for whom the sign was meant,
And in his hand she laid her own, and smiled.

XI.

The next day, Richard Wain, when riding past,
Heard Ruth's bird-voice trilling in the lane,
And caught a glimpse of her between the trees,
A picture, for an instant, in a frame.
He thought, "The prize I coveted is near;

She will be mine before the set of sun."
Returning soon, toward the house he went,
Strode to the door, calling for Dalton Earl,
And told him for what merchandise he came.
The girl was not for sale, the other said.
"You talk at random now," said Richard Wain,
"You know I hold the deed of all your lands,
And so, unless you let the woman go,
Your whole estate shall have a sheriff's sale."
The planter turned a coward at the threat,
And knowing well what blood ran in the veins
Of her he sold, reluctant gave consent.

Above his wine he told Ruth of her fate,
And to the floor she fell, and swooned away.
Recovering, she rose upon her knees,
And begged, and prayed, that she might still remain.
At this he told her how the lands were held,
And if she went not he must starve or beg.
"Then let the lands be sold, and sold again;
If his, they are not yours. What good will come
If I do go to him? then all is his.
Last night I gave my hand to Karagwe.
O, it will break my heart to go away."
Lightly his mustache twirled Dalton Earl.

At dusk, in tears to Karagwe's low roof,
Ruth passed, and uttered, with wild, angry words,
The hard conditions that had been imposed.
She wept; he comforted: "There yet was hope;

There was a Hero, in a Book he read,
Who said that those who suffered would be blessed."
Then for the last, toward the planter's house
They walked, and o'er them saw the spider moon
Weaving the storm upon its web of cloud.

XII.

But Karagwe, when once he turned again,
Smote wildly his infuriated breast.
His fierce eyes flashed; he thirsted for revenge.
Then came a calmer mood, and far away
Sped the expelled thoughts like shuddering gusts of
wind.
He wept that this injustice should be done;
Yet knew that in God's hand the scale was set,
And though His poor, down-trodden, waited long,
They waited surely, for His hour would come.

XIII.

The night passed, and the troublous morning broke,
And Ruth was sold away from him she loved.

The dark day died, and when the moon arose,
The foremost torch in day's long funeral train,
Karagwe went down toward the river's brink,
Thinking of what had been. He turned and saw
His enemy walk calmly up the road.
Quickly behind him came another form;

And in a jeweled hand, half raised to strike,
A poniard glistened. Then the negro rose,
And caught the weapon from the assassin's grasp,
And stood before the planter, Dalton Earl!
"Forgive," he said, "Forgiveness is a slave;
She has no pride, she never does an ill;
For she is meekly great, and nobly good,
And patient, though the lash of anger smites."

Rebuked, the master stood before the slave,
And Richard Wain passed on, nor knew his life
Was saved by one that he had that day wronged.
Thus Dalton Earl: "I thank you for this act,
Thwarting a bad intent. Yet I had cause
To take the sullied life of Richard Wain.
He drugged the wine he gave me at his house,
And knowing that I had with me the deed
And title of my lands, begged me to play,
And while I played, stake all upon a card.
He won, and I have hated from that hour."

XIV.

Like some great thought that finds release at last,
The happy Spring in buds expression found.

Coralline Earl grew rich in every grace.
Her eyes' blue heavens were serene with soul,
And goodness sunned her face from light within.
Her hands were soft with kindness. On her brow
Shone hope, more lovely than a ruby star.

As in the ancient days sat Mordecai
At the king's gate, and waited for the hour,
When, clothed with pomp, he too should take his seat
Among the mighty nobles of the land,
So at the gateway of her palace heart,
Love tarried, that he too might enter in,
And rule the kingdom of another life.

Not long the waiting; for when Stanley Thane
Came from his northern home with Dalton Earl,
And on the terrace steps met Coralline,
Love took the sceptre that his waiting won.

Well worthy to be loved was Stanley Thane.
He could not claim a titled ancestor,
Nor boast of any blood but Puritan.
His father was successful on exchange,
Reaped fortune by a rise in merchandise,
Now sent his partner son with Dalton Earl
Toward the claspless girdle of the South.
And Stanley Thane was all that makes true men;
High thought, high purpose, loving right the best,
His mind was clear and fresh as air at morn.

He kissed the rosy tips of Coralline's hand,
And that day galloped with her through the town,
And wandered with her down magnolia lanes,
And watched, below the spray-woofed fall, the brook,
That seemed a maid, who, sitting at a loom,
Wove misty lace to decorate the rocks.

XV.

Long o'er his writings hidden in the tree
Pondered the slave, and found at last their worth.
Must he return them? To whom did they belong?
If he should give them back to Dalton Earl
Unjustly, Richard Wain might claim them still.
He chose to keep them folded round the Book,
Hid in the secret hollow of the tree.

He thought of Ruth as one who was at rest,
And wept for her as though she was no more,
And sometimes gathered flowers, and placed them
where
He knew she soon would pass, as tenderly
As though he laid them down upon her grave.

XVI.

Once in the twilight, as the shadows fell,
A skiff shot from the under-reaching shore,
And Stanley Thane and Coralline sailed down
The languid waters, 'neath the dappled moon.
They spoke of giant wars that yet might be
To drive the dragon Slavery from the land.
Coralline smoothed the evils it had wrought.
Stanley, who could not see a wrong excused,
Said, "God is just; he knows nor white nor black.
If war must come, each shackle will be forced,
To make, at last, the nation wholly free."

And Karagwe, who pulled a silent oar,
Shut the winged words in cages of his heart;
But Coralline was angry at the speech,
And rained disdain on noble Stanley's head,
Scorning his Northern thought and Northern blood,
And sighed that it had been their lot to meet.
"If that is true," he said, "then let us part,
And let us hope we shall not meet again.
Adieu! for I shall see you never more."

The boat was near the bank; he sprang to it,
And left her sitting in the gilded prow—
Her pride, a raging Hector of the hour,
Fighting a thousand tears, whose war-cry rose:
Thin patience brings thick damage in the end.

XVII.

When Richard Wain found that the deed was lost,
Which he had won at play with Dalton Earl,
Chagrin and rage were ready at a beck,
Like waters in a dam, to pass the race,
And turn the voluble mill-wheel of his tongue.
He half suspected Dalton Earl the thief,
Yet knew, if this were true, the threat he made
To gain Ruth from him, would have been in vain.
And so, because he feared to lose his power,
He kept his secret that the deed was lost.

PART SECOND.

Now through the mighty pulses of the land
Throbbed the dark blood of war; and Sumter's guns
Were the first heart-beats of a better day.
The avenging angel, with a scourging sword
Of fire and death, with triumph on his face,
Swept o'er the nation with the cry of War!
Ten thousand boroughs, dreaming peace, awake.
War in the South, with the South! War! War!
The shame we nourished stings us to the death.

O, fair, false wife, South! lo, thy lord, the North,
Loveth thee still, though thou hast gone astray.
In truth's great court, vain has thy trial been,
For no divorce could there be granted thee.
The child you bore was bitter curse and shame,
And not the child of thy husband, the North.
It has led thee to miry paths, and raised
The gall of despair to thy famished lips;
It were better that such a child should die.

I.

The first year of the war had passed away
When Richard Wain, the planter, sprang to arms.
The day for his departure had been set;
To-morrow it would be, and as the night
Fell on the misty hills, and on the vales,
He sat alone in his accustomed room;

Thinking, he drowsed; his chin couched on his breast;
A dim light wrought at shadows on the walls.
Slowly the sash was raised behind him there.
Perhaps he slept; he did not heed the noise,
And Karagwe sprang in, and faced his foe.
He held a long knife up and brandished it,
And said, "As surely as you call or move,
Your life will not be worth a blade of grass;
But if you do not call, and sign the words,
That I have written on a paper here,
No harm will come, and I shall go away."
He drew the paper forth; the planter read:
I promise if the deed is ever found
Of Dalton Earl's estate, I in no way
Shall lay a claim to it to make it mine.
I here surrender all my right to it.

"Why, this I shall not sign, of course," he said.
"You might have asked me to give back your Ruth,
And I would not have minded; but your game
Lies deeper than a check upon the queen."

"Sign!" cried the negro; and at Ruth's name,
A sudden madness leaped along his nerves,
Like flame among the dry prairie grass.
"Sign! for unless you sign this writing now,
You shall not live; now promise me to sign!"
He caught the planter fiercely by the throat,
Starting his quailing eyes, "Now will you sign or not?
You have ten seconds more to make your choice."

"Give me the paper then, and I will sign."
The name was written, and the negro went;
But not an hour had passed, before the hounds
Of Richard Wain and Dalton Earl were slipped,
And scenting on his track through stream and field.

II.

The slave first ran toward the hollow tree;
There left the paper signed by Richard Wain,
Disturbing not the deed; but took the Book,
And up the tireless road, fled on and on,
Until he gained the borders of a marsh.

The night was dark, but darker still the clouds
That loomed along the rim where day had gone.
The wind blew cold, and hastened quickly past,
Escaping, like a slave, the hound-like clouds
Whose thunder-barkings sounded in its ears.

And Karagwe had only reached the marsh,
When on his track he heard the savage dogs.
He knew the paths and windings many miles,
And even in the darkness found his way,
And gained a covert island, where a hut,
Built by some poor and friendless fugitive,
Afforded shelter and secure abode.
He tarried here until along the hills
The red-lipped whisper of the morning ran.
Then, when he would have ventured from the door,

A large black hound arose, and licked his hand.
The dog was Dalton Earl's ; he started back.

The dream of freedom nourished many years
Seemed withering, and for the moment lost.
For long the slave had thought of liberty,
And worshipped her, as in that elder time
A tyrant's subjects worshipped, praying her
That she would not delay, but hasten forth,
And bridge the hated gulf 'twixt rich and poor,
By freeing all the mass from ignorance,
By lifting up the worthy of the earth,
And making knowledge paramount to wealth.

III.

O strange, that in our age, and in a land
Where liberty was laid the corner-stone,
A slave, perforce, should be obliged to dream,
And dote on freedom, like the poor oppressed
Who lived and hoped two thousand years ago!

And slavery to this slave was like a fruit —
A bitter and a hateful fruit to taste —
The fruit of error and of ignorance,
Made rank with superstition and with crime.

Yet though the fruit was bitter to the core,
Many there were who died for love of it.
O, many they who listen through long nights

To hear a footstep that will never come.
There is not a flower along the border blown,
From Lookout Mountain to the Chesapeake,
But has in it the blood of North and South.

IV.

Karagwe went back, and on a paper wrote, —
"Your dog has harmed me not, and why should
you,
That I have never wronged, plot harm to me?
You made me slave, you sold away my bride,
And now you set your hounds upon my track,
Because I seek the freedom that is mine.
Though you have wronged me, still I do you good,
For in an oak, the largest of the grove,
Upon the cotton-field of Richard Wain,
Hid in a hollow near the second limb,
Is the lost deed that holds your house and lands."
The paper fastened round the hound's strong neck,
The negro bade him go, and forth he went;
And Earl read what the slave had written down,
And that day found the deed hid in the tree,
And that day ceased pursuing any more.

For two long weeks the negro in the swamps
Wandered toward the North, living at times
On berries and on fruit. Above him leaned
The tall trees, bower-like 'neath their wrestling arms;
Beneath, the murky waters, black as death,

Stirred only to the plunge of venomed things.
The long, seared grasses clung to every bough
Whose trailing robe hung near the sluggish lymph.
And here and there, among the savage moss,
Blossomed alone some snowy gold-spired flower,
Like God's own church found in a heathen land.
The birds o'erhead, that, plumaged like the morn,
Caroled their sweetness, sang the holy psalms.

V.

But now across his path the negro found
A belt of water falling with the tide.
Two heavy logs he lashed, and launched them out,
Then, with a pole for help in case of need,
Sprang on the float, and drifted down the stream.
Thus for two days he drifted, eating naught
Except the berries growing near the shore.
Then on a cool, bright morning, when the wind
And tide agreed, he saw again the sea.
Far off a buoy was tossing on the waves,
Much like the red heart of the joyful deep —
Much like a heart upon a sea of life;
And ships were in the offing, sailing on
Like the vague ships that with our hopes and fears
Put from their harbors to return no more.

VI.

The raft went oceanward. The negro raised
Upon the pole the coat that he had worn,

Hoping for succor from the distant ships;
And not in vain; for ere the sun had set,
Half starved, he clambered up a vessel's side,
And found himself with friends, and on his way
To freedom, 'neath the steadfast northern star.

VII.

Two years of war, two years of many tears,
And Richard Wain, a captain of renown,
In ranks led on by error, fought and fell.

Within the breast of Coralline, Stanley Thane
Possessed acknowledged empire; all her love
Was poured out on him, and her heart
Stood like an emptied vase. Then from the North
Came rumors of his daring, and the war
Gloomed like a night about her, — he its star.

VIII.

The golden spirit in each lily bloom,
That, pollen-vestured, laughs at care all day
Had closed the doors and shutters of its house.
Forth in the dewy garden, 'neath the stars,
Walked Coralline and Ruth, sad and alone;
For Ruth was owned again by Dalton Earl.

"I grieve," said Coralline, "that Stanley Thane
Left me so rashly, and that he thinks

My hasty words were said with earnest thought.
Would that a bird might fly to him and sing —
'She loves you still, Stanley, she loves you still.'"

Ruth followed quickly, "Your wish is heard;
For I will go to him who once was here,
And say to him the words that you have said."
Then fell the other on the quadroon's neck,
And kissed her through her tears, and promised her
Her freedom, if she went to Stanley Thane.
She did not dream what impulse urged the slave,
Nor that in sending her toward the North
Bearing a message full of trust and love,
She sent a message smeared with blood instead.

For Ruth hoped now for vengeance for her past.
Wronged by her father, she would wreak her hate
Full on her sister, and destroy her peace,
As hers had been destroyed in dark dead days.

IX.

That night she stole a knife, and sharpened it,
And while she drew it up and down the stone,
Sipped from the poison nectar of revenge.
She thought of Stanley Thane, and pitied him
That he should be the victim of her hate;
But wished that Coralline could see him then,
After the violent knife had done its work,
Laid out and ready for his last abode.

X.

So Ruth arose, and when the wine-lipped Dawn,
Gathering his robes about him like a god,
Went up to the great summits of the world
From the black valleys of immeasurable space,
She passed beyond the limit of the vale.

Those she loved best had all been torn away;
The last, her child, was sold she knew not where;
And Coralline too should taste a bitter cup,
Feeling the fury of a deep revenge.

XI.

For many days Ruth journeyed to the North,
And reached at last the camp. She passed the guard,
And in the night discovered Stanley's tent;
Then gliding in, bent o'er him while he slept.
He dreamed of Coralline, and in his sleep
Said — "Coralline, 'tis better to forgive."
And Ruth who heard, cried, "She forgives;
She loves you still, Stanley — she loves you still!"
At this he woke, and saw the woman there,
And saw the weapon raised above his breast,
And a vague horror at the mockery of the words
Left him all powerless, and sealed up his speech.
But one swift hand passed in and grasped the arm,
And snatched the knife, and there before them stood
Karagwe, with Ruth Earl face to face.

XII.

And after, at Fort Pillow, when the storm
Had gone against us, and the traitors slew
Five hundred men who had laid down their arms,
Karagwe was shot, and with a prayer
For his whole country, he fell back and died.

Some, seeking the highest type of noble men,
Compare their heroes with the cavaliers,
Boasting their ancestry through tangled lines;
But I, who care not for patrician blood,
Hold him the highest who constrains great ends,
Or rounds a prudent life with noble deeds.

DEMETRIUS.

I.

THE SUCCESS OF THE BEGGAR.

IN my life I have had two idols, one my country, one my wife,
And I know I loved them faithfully, and both with one accord;
But the day came, beaded falsely on my brittle leash of life,
When perforce I chose between them, through the wisdom of the Lord.

High upon the rocky summit of a cliff in red Algiers,
Raised against the sky of sunset, like a beaker filled with wine,
While each dome is like a bubble that above the brim appears,
Stands the city I was born in, my belovèd Constantine.

Nobly rise the brick-roofed houses with their heavy gray stone walls,

While here and there, above them all, the mosque and minaret;
Like the voice of some enchanter sounds the bearded muezzin's calls,
And the rustle of the cypress seems a murmur of regret.

Round the ancient Cintran city runs a dark wall broad and strong,
Like the mailed belt of a warrior, and the gate the buckle seems;
While a tower toward the sunset is a dagger hilted long;
Whose blade is hid in foldings of a circling sash of streams.

Far away the Atlas mountains rear their heads of lasting snow,
And seem like old men grouped around in high-backed chairs of space;
And they bathe their feet like children in the brooks that run below,
Or smoke their pipes in silence till the clouds obscure each face.

I was poor: they say they found me lying naked in the street,
And a beggar so befriended me and brought me to his door,

And cared for me and tended me, until my growing feet
Could patter through the market-place and there increase our store.

I never knew the tenderness of father or of mother;
My tatters scarcely covered me; my hunger made me thin;
I never knew of sympathy or kindness from another;
I drank the cup of bitterness that comes to want and sin.

All my early youth was squandered, when there came across my thought
A passionate intolerance of the course my life had run;
And I went out to the venders and some meagre fruitage bought,
Till with selling and with buying, lo, a new life was begun.

Soon I found myself the owner of vast houses, wares, and sails,
A very prince of traffic, with my slaves beyond the line,
Where they sold my costly merchandise of cloth and cotton bales,
Of many colored leathers, ostrich feathers, dates, and wine.

II.

THE MAIDEN OF THE GOLDEN KIOSK.

In the days when I, a beggar, wandered idly through the street,
Past the palace, through the vineyards where the scented fountains play,
Standing near the golden kiosk, it befell my lot to meet
One for whom my heart grew larger, and I could not turn away.

Long my eyes upon the banquet of her beauty freely fed;
How could I help but love her, whom the angels might adore!
But at last, tired of my staring, she turned away her head;
Yet I saw the large pearls tremble that about her neck she wore.

Either cheek was sea-shell tinted, and around her dewy lips
Played a smile that lingered lovingly, like star gleam on the sea;
Thus emboldened, on my knees I fell, and kissed her finger tips,
And begged of her, and prayed of her that I her slave might be.

I was dark and swarthy featured, comely still in form and face;
My long black hair hung glossily about my neck and head;
My large jet eyes were lustrous, and I had an easy grace
That almost made a kingly robe my ragged garb of red.

I chained the maiden with my arm, I would not let her go;
She said she was Eudocia, that Yorghi was her sire;
I said I was Demetrius, a beggar vile and low,
But 'neath my heart's one crucible love lit its fusing fire.

Her sensuous long dark lashes hung above her dreamy eyes,
Like twin clouds of stormy portent balanced over limpid deeps;
Like the wings of birds of passage seen against the hazy skies;
Like the petal o'er the pollen of the flow'ret when it sleeps.

All her vesture was embroidered with the finest lace of gold;
A diamond in her turban with its eye-like glitter shone;

The white dress more than half revealed a form of perfect mould,
And her cincture, dagger-fastened, shaped the garment to her zone.

To my eyes she gave her dark eyes, down to gaze into and dream;
And I seemed like one who leans above a bridge's slender rail,
And thinks, and gazes wistfully deep down into the stream,
While the twilight gathers round him, and the gleam-winged stars prevail.

After this I met her daily in the palace-garden ways,
And she always came to meet me, and opened wide the gate,
Often chiding, often smiling at my minute-long delays,
And bringing dainty viands in a golden cup and plate.

I, her lover, was a beggar, but she loved me all the same;
Had I been Haroun Alraschid she could not have loved me more;
While she whispered, on my lips and on my eyes she kissed my name,
And vined her arms about my neck; how could I but adore?

But all pleasure cloys or ceases; if the cup is stricken down,
All its contents are like acid, burning deep a long regret;
If it cloys, we calmly leave it, with perhaps a careless frown,
Or may be a pleasant memory that is easy to forget.

Once when in the golden kiosk, with Eudocia's hand in mine,
Came old Yorghi frowning darkly with the storm upon his face;
Would she bring disgrace upon him? Would she break his noble line?
He stamped his fierce invective, and he drove me from the place.

Ere I went I turned upon him, and I boldly claimed her hand,
And vowed that I would have her, though the city barred my way;
But he scoffed at me, a beggar, and repeated his command,
Never more to meet his daughter, for my life's sake, from that day.

III.

THE VISIT OF DEMETRIUS AND HIS TEN FRIENDS.

So two lives, like confluent rivers, were unkindly torn apart;
One to slide through fruited gardens, longing vainly for the sea,
One to purl 'neath ample bridges, bearing cargoes to the mart,
But ever dreaming fondly of a meeting yet to be.

And I labored; and my gains accrued and doubled in my hand,
For Fortune having given once will give us more and more;
I was like a stranger passing through some long neglected land,
Who finds beneath each stone he turns a wedge of golden ore.

And I studied, learned all secrets that the wisest books can teach;
Gained the Greek verb's long persistent root at last by prying hard;
Found a natural foreknowledge of the rules and forms of speech,
And drank the fountain water from the words of Scio's bard.

All my ships had favoring breezes, not one sank or
went ashore;
The very fat of commerce oozed between their
pitchy seams;
And a block of serried buildings did not half contain my store,
While my lavish, thrifty bargains would have
dimmed Aladdin's dreams.

Still I changed not my apparel, still I wore my bezan robe,
Still I donned the self-same turban with its frayed
and faded red;
I would have no other garb then had I owned the
whirling globe;
Better rich to wear a tatter, than poor, wear silk,
I said.

Daily from my mullioned window flew a pigeon in
the air,
And beneath its wing lay folded lines for her I
loved the best;
Daily from her palace window it returned and
brought me there,
Rhymeless idyls full of heart-speech, faithful ardors of her breast.

Ah, dear love, she waited patiently with mournful,
longing eyes,
Like the moon she waited nightly for the cloud
to pass her brow;

Like the birds she waited daily for the coming in the skies
Of the other bringing succor to the hunger on the bough.

And all wealth was lost upon her, for she had to look upon
Art's own pictures, Spring-time raptures, Autumn clad in ballet mist;
And she dined on sweets and spices, coffee, bread and cinnamon,
While they shook perfumes about her, or her cushioned slippers kissed.

Down her back her hair, unfastened from its jeweled comb of gold,
Wasted fragrance, seemed a cascade plunging down a deep ravine;
Seemed the black wing of a raven who had ventured overbold,
And was perched upon her forehead that its beauty might be seen.

Every day in milk she bathed her, till at last she was as white;
Dyed with almond kohl her eyelids, and her nails with henna tinged;
Supped on amber wine and honey; but she tasted no delight.
She slept 'neath silken curtains with musk-scented laces fringed.

But at last the ready day came, that my hopes had longed to meet,
When I cast aside the tatters I had worn for many years,
And arrayed my perfect person from my head down to my feet,
With the garments that became me, with the velvet of my peers.

Then I bought me restless chargers, Ukraine steeds, five white, six black;
The eleventh was the noblest, yet the gentlest of all;
And a friend I had who loved me to bestride each horse's back —
Ten friends of handsome presence, smooth demeanor, strong, and tall.

Every friend I gave a cloak to, purple velvet ermine-bound;
Every charger was caparisoned — the harness wrought with gold.
At high noon we started gayly, and the palace entrance found;
And I sought the statesman Yorghi with a purpose to unfold.

I had come to wed his daughter; all her heart had long been mine;
I had won her when a beggar, but I loved her more and more

Now that my wealth was boundless — it but strengthened my design;
If he gave her I would cede him half my fortune, store on store.

In my face he laughed, me scorning, and despised me and my part —
Called me still a beggar wealthy, and bade me turn away;
Said Eudocia was his daughter — he knew nothing of her heart;
He had pledged her hand and fortune to my ruler, Ahmed Bey.

There are times when our resentment centres solely in a glance,
When our feelings burn too deeply for effectiveness in speech;
Such a look I gave to Yorghi as I led out in advance,
While my ten friends followed after with brave consolation each.

IV.

DEMETRIUS FOR EUDOCIA BETRAYS CONSTANTINE.

Now a war like distant thunder muttered in the darkened air;
In the sky a fowl of omen hovered o'er to rob our graves;

And men, like birds affrighted, hurried homeward in despair.
We heard the tramp of armies like the far-off march of waves.

War a pestilent disease is on the body of the world —
A disease that sometimes purges, but still leaves the victim sore;
And no potent drug will cure it until Liberty has furled
All the standards of the nations, and shall rule for evermore.

What availed my marble buildings where I bartered for my gold?
All my gains were vainly gotten, for Eudocia was not mine.
Then my goods I turned to money, all my ships and houses sold,
And sent the glittering product far away from Constantine.

On us like a wild hawk swooping came Damrémont with his men;
But we saw his wing-like banners and we closed and barred the gates;
All the women urged to battle; every man a hero then;
And the Kabyles based reliance on the friendship of the Fates.

I held that love of country was a higher love of self,
With generous ends, but selfish still, whatever might be said;
I forgot my boasted honor; I had garnered all my pelf;
I became a hissing traitor to the land I owed my bread.

All was plain; if I was faithful, then Eudocia was lost;
Recreant, and gaining victory, I could claim her as my right.
I scarcely weighed the balance, and I dared not count the cost;
I stole out from the city to the alien camp that night.

I was loyal to the purpose that within my heart was shrined;
Another might have coped with it, and triumphed o'er its fall.
So men are, they do not vary much, the level of mankind,
What one lacks the next possesses; there are faults enough in all.

Down the cliff I slipped in silence; and the troubled cypress leaves
Quivered like sweet lips in anguish, while the star eyes wept with dew;

And I sought the French commander, where, amid his musket sheaves,
He sat and planned new reaping in a field that Azrael knew.

"I have come to bring assistance, if you take my terms," I said,
"For I know the weakest portion of the city's scowling wall.
There's a maiden named Eudocia I would sell my soul to wed;
Give me the right to have her, and I freely tell you all."

Then he smiled across his table as he granted my desire —
Smile of memory begotten, some remembrance of delight —
And he heard my story quietly, but said he would require
Me to go into the city as a spy the coming night.

V.

THE MASKED SPY IN THE PALACE.

Years before, a secret entrance 'neath the wall I ordered made;
And they were dead who built it, so none knew of it but me.

When the darkness came I gained it, and softly in the shade,
 Passed through lone streets of the city where the battle was to be.

A purse of gold and rubies bought the whispered countersign,
 And with its aid I noted place and number of the troops.
I chalked upon a building: *Lo, the doom of Constantine!*
 There 's a traitor in the city, and the populace are dupes.

In the street I met a masker hurrying onward through the night,
 And something in his bearing told of one I called a friend.
"Sir," I said, and on his shoulder I had laid my finger quite,
 "Tell me why you mask your visage, and whereto your footsteps tend."

By my voice he knew me quickly, and removed his mask to say:
 "My footsteps seek the palace; have you heard not of the fête?
In three days old Yorghi's daughter is to wed with Ahmed Bey;
 To-night the plighting party; I must hasten; it is late."

"Hold," I said, "you care but little for the pleasure
that you seek;
Give to me your mask and vesture, and so let
me take your place;
I shall not hold the favor lightly, but shall pay you
in a week
With a sapphire for each moment; and they will
not see my face.

Then we found his wide apartments, where we
changed the robes we wore.
I put on the half fantastic silken garments and
the mask,
Then sallied down the stair-way till I gained the
street once more;
Dreaming only of Eudocia, in whose presence I
should bask.

From foundation to entablature the palace shone
with light,
And I fancied it a genii with a hundred fiery
eyes;
His mouth the yawning door-way, and a cloud across
the night
Seemed the hair upon his forehead, blowing in the
windy skies.

Quick he gorged me, for I entered, and heard at
once the swell
Of the music — heard the dancing girls with bells
about their feet;

The odor of a hundred blooms upon my senses fell;
  The magnolia seemed the husband, and the rest his consorts sweet.

To a splendid hall a eunuch led me down a damask floor,
  And the guests were all assembled in their beauty and their pride.
With standards and with banners the walls were garnished o'er.
  The Bey among the maskers led the lily by his side.

Round a fountain, in the centre of the golden burnished room,
  Danced the dancers, played the players, to the cadence of its fall,
While out upon the balcony, amid the vernal gloom,
  A nightingale was singing, and with sadness mocked us all.

VI.

THE MEETING IN THE GARDEN, AND THE FLIGHT OF THE SPY.

When the Bey passed by me graciously, I whispered in the ear
  Of the one he led beside him (should I fail to win her yet!)

"Our day is at its dawning; I, Demetrius, am here;
Meet me yonder in the garden, at the place where once we met."

There she followed very quickly, and I held her to my heart,
And kissed with fervid kisses all her lips and throat and chin.
Here she longed to dwell forever so that we might never part,
And be fed with many kisses my enfolding arms within.

There the amorous stars out-twinkled; and anear, a sordid lake,
Like a miser, hugged the silver of their glitter to its breast;
And it stayed within the closet of the trees and tangled brake,
Lest some fortunate bold robber should steal from it in its rest.

Now the years had changed Eudocia from the rose-bud to the rose,
Made more perfect every feature, added many a gentle grace,
And she made my heart her garden, there to dwell and find repose:
Neither time, nor change, nor absence, could her love for me efface.

She said she too would be a lakelet, 'neath the starlight of my eyes;
And when my lips bent downward she would catch their spicy dew;
My face, low bending over, should become her tender skies,
And my arms the goodly verdure that about the margin grew.

I dared not risk to tell her of the traitor she was near;
I said the Bey would tremble when I came to claim her hand;
I said that she must wait me, and despair not; but have cheer,
For my triumph would be public in the corners of the land.

While we spoke we heard commotion in the palace down the hill;
Gay lights swung in the distance, like red fire-flies in a glen;
Call by call was heard and answered with a herd of echoes shrill,
And we saw a score of torches, and the issuing forth of men.

"Love, they seek you," cried Eudocia; "you must go or you must die."
But sad, O, sad the sundering of two hearts who long and weep;

Rent the oak's tough, knitted fibre by the lightning
from on high;
But the hearts will cling the closer that apart
they strive to keep.

On her lips I kissed my tears in, on her lips and
on her eyes
Which she opened only languidly to show her an-
swering tears,
And I kissed the diamond crescent that I saw sink
down and rise,
While it flashed upon the torches with a hundred
silver spears.

Swooning, on a seat I laid her, then sped quickly
through the gloom,
While a torchman passed so near me that I fan-
cied I was seen;
But I hid me for a moment 'neath a bush of liberal
bloom,
Then fled onward to my entrance through the
streets that intervene.

Above, an imminent meteor flashed westward 'gainst
the night, —
A full moon with a bluer glow, and trailed with
ruby shine;
It seemed a blazing torch to me, borne onward with
the flight
Of a spirit, that beneath it, brought defeat to
Constantine.

VII.

THE BATTLE.

To the town outspoke the cannon, ere the dawn charged on the night,
  Not of peace and joy and amity, but of hatred and despair,
And a thousand blatant bugles proved it waiting for their spite;
  And we heard the rasp of bullets in the dark astonished air.

When the sun rose, hot and bloody, all the fight had well begun;
  The artillery were pounding at the weak place in the wall;
While the smoke, from vale and city, seemed the melancholy, dun
  Robes of spirits hovering over for the fated ones to fall.

Like a strong Numidian lion, on her rock the city lay,
  Nothing daunted though surrounded, and with scanty store of bread;
Her fierce eyes, two flags of crimson, stared through battle all the day,
  One on Babel Wad's high key-stone, and one on Babel Djed.

Round these gates they set their sworders, hoping thence to drive us back
When we followed up their sallies, which were baits to make us come;
But in vain, our works were safer, though we longed for the attack,
And eagerly awaited for the summons of the drum.

Stone by stone a breach was opened in the thin place in the wall,
Till at last we sent a truce flag to the gate of Babel Djed,
Saying to the town, "Surrender, Constantine must surely fall;
If you fail, no soul remaining shall be left to count your dead."

Like a sword-thrust was the answer, "There is plenty in the place
Both of food and ammunition; if 'tis these the French desire,
We can furnish them abundance; but surrender means disgrace,
And our homes shall be defended while one soldier stands to fire."

Should not this town be captured, every man must bear the fault,
And many a one bethought him of his own in sunny France.

Down our line there ran the murmur, " We must take it by assault,"
And we heard the bugles playing for the stormers to advance.

Like great billows never breaking were the rocks of Constantine,
And a cargoed ship the city with its keel in every one;
She was sailing for the future with the barter of the line,
And her mast-like towers were gaudy with the pennons of the sun.

But now a storm had struck her, and a hole was in her side,
And the waters rushed in wildly while she paused upon the brink.
All in vain each brave endeavor; for all on board her tried
To close the leak with fury, that the vessel might not sink.

Our men the angry waters that could not be turned nor checked,
And they bore all straws before them in their mad impetuous way.
So the town, betrayed, was captured; so the great ship had been wrecked;
And with the troops in triumph I rode in upon that day.

VIII.

THE WEDDING AND THE FALSE FRIEND.

When the night fell, in the palace all the lights were lit again.
In the hall of silken standards and of Persia-woven mats
There were women fair as houris, there were brave and handsome men;
And the fish leaped up to see them from the fountain's silver vats.

Never yet so fair Eudocia, and she won the wisest praise
From the aliens there assembled to behold our marriage rite;
Not alone her queenly beauty; but the grace of all her ways,
Drew all hearts and eyes toward her, filled like cups with pure delight.

But while yet they said the service, and ere yet I placed the ring
On her tapering heart finger, all the crowd was parted wide,
And I saw my friend the masker his unasked-for presence bring
To the pollen of the wedding, lady-petaled on each side.

"Thus shall die the thankless traitor, whether king or beggar he!"
And a dagger gleamed above us with a fierce glare at the light,
Then was struck upon my bosom near the place the heart might be,
And my false friend, through the people, hastened wildly in his flight.

But the mad bee gained no honey in his hurry to depart;
His sting had been well pointed, but his villainy was loss,
For I wore, with faith, a secret, o'er the throbbing of my heart,
The symbol of a higher life, a simple silver Cross.

This had turned aside the weapon and spared me many years
For one whose heart has been to me a holy pilgrim shrine,
For one for whom I gave away with bitterness and tears
The city of Jugurtha, my own mother Constantine.

We dwell now in a palace near the white surge of a bay;
But at times my good steed wanders, and in the twilight late,

I find me near my city, while the muezzin in the gray,
Shouts, "To prayer, to prayer, ye people, only God is good and great!"

THE STRONG SPIDER.

I.

THE CHIEF'S DAUGHTER.

I WAS a naturalist, and had crossed the sea
And come to Theodosia, to find
A monstrous spider of which I had heard.
The people of the town wagged doubting heads,
When asked about it; but one day I met
A sturdy fisherman who once had seen
The spider, though he knew not his abode.
He said the spider was as long as he,
And that the woof whereof he wove his web,
Was thick as any cordage on his boat.
At night, belated 'mid the tumuli
That mound the hill-side and the vernal vale,
Like the raised letters of an ancient page
Made for the blind gropers of to-day to read,
He entered a dark tomb, and therein slept,
Until the world, like some round shield upraised,
Splintered the thrown spears of dawn. As he
woke,
He found himself ensnared in some thick web,
Yet reached his knife, and slowly cut it through;
Then when he stood, a monstrous spider fled.

At this recital on the slanted shore,
Another joined us from the cottage near—
A vine-clad cottage, fit for love's abode.
A lily-croft, with trees, encinctured it;
Like Ahab in his house of ivory
Dining on sweets, the king bee here
Sipped in the snowy lily's palace hall;
And here were yellow lilies strewn about,
As though the place had been the banquet grove
Of Shishak, king of Egypt; for the flowers
Seemed like the cups of gold that Solomon
Wrought for the holy service of the Lord.

"This is my daughter," said the fisherman.
Her head and face were covered with a scarf,
But large dark eyes looked forth, and in their depths
I saw a soul all tenderness and truth.

(Often, in dreams, I thought it sweet to die,
And reft of this gross vision, see at last,
As the large soul, quit of the body can,
Another soul set free and purified.)

The modest maid a crimson jacket wore,
And to her knee the broidered skirt hung down;
While 'neath, the Turkish garment was confined
In plaits about the ankles; but her shoes
Revealed the naked insteps of her feet.
I bade her there adieu, upon the shore

Of the clear Bospore. As I wandered back,
I thought much of the spider that I sought;
But more of two dark eyes, that seemed two stars
Which shone down in my heart; while the far space
Behind them, pure, but unknown, was the soul.

I thought to test this maiden's charity;
And so, one friendly day, put on a robe
Tattered and soiled with use. As she went by,
I strode abruptly from behind a wall,
And faced her with a face disguised, and held
My hand out while I begged for some small alms.
She gave abundantly from her lean purse,
And with a look of tender pity, passed.
It matters little who it is that asks,
Or whether he deserves the alms or not;
That given with free heart, is given to God,
And not to him who takes.

Day after day,
Henceforth, I strode a coastward way, to meet
The dark-eyed daughter of the fisherman.
Beneath her roof she made my welcome sweet,
And yielded both her hands, and drew the scarf
That veiled the wondrous beauty of her face.
If painter, or if sculptor, in some dream,
Could mingle Faith with Love and Charity,
And give them utterance in one pure face,
I know the face would be a face like hers.

Her eyes were diamond doors of her true soul,
And with their silken latches softly closed,
When, couched beneath his poppy parachute,
Inactive Sleep came by. Her glances seemed
Like gold-winged angels sent from heavenly doors.
Yet she was often sad when I was near.
Once, tarrying late, I told her of my life,
And of the monster I had come to find;
But now, lo! she around my heart had wound
The close web of her love, and held me fast
As any fly caught in a spider's toils.

Clothed in the sackcloth of regret, she said,
She long had wept the past; but for my sake
She now would cast it off, and live for me.

I said that few could exculpate the past
From stormy doing with the ships of hope.

She said it made her sad to think upon
Their present dwindled fortune, and the yoke
Her people chafed their necks in, on the hills.
Her father was a brave Circassian chief;
But here he dwelt disguised, till once again
He could lead on his race, and wound the heel
That ground them to the dust.

Our hearts made new,
We kissed good-night, and parted. As I went,
A distant hill, all shadow, took new shape,

And seemed a sprawling spider, while two trees
That grew upon it, were his upraised arms
Clutching at two red fire-flies, that were stars.

II.

THE SPIDER.

With day-break came a knuckle at my door;
I rose, and opened, and upon the porch,
His face like strange death's, and his dark eyes
wide
With some vague horror, stood the fisherman.
"Come, hasten with me," were his only words.
We ran our best along the barren shore,
And gained his silent cottage. Entering,
He led me to his daughter's vacant couch.
The room had but one window, and the sash
Was raised. I looked out to the ground beneath.
A vine crept up, and with long fingers made
Abode secure upon the cottage side,
And o'er the window threw a leafy scarf.
But what was this, that fastened to the ledge
Trailed to the ground? A glutinous rope
Twisted with five strands. This the fisherman
Saw with new horror, while between white lips
He gasped, "The Spider!"

What was best to do?
We saw strange foot-prints on the moistened beach,
But these were lost soon in a wooded dell

Where all trace had an end. The long day through
We sought among the tombs, up from the dell;
But unrewarded, when the sun was quenched,
Sat down to weep. So darkness dropped,
And like an awful spider, o'er the earth
Crawled with gaunt legs of shadow. Then our
    homes
We sadly sought, to meet again at morn.

The night was warm, and with my window raised,
I sat and mourned, and wrung my hopeless hands.
No light was in the house. I half reclined —
My back toward the window. Something shut
The puny sheen of starlight from the room.
The Thing, a monstrous shape, was with me there,
And two hard arms were thrown about my waist.
For very terror I was hushed, nor moved
To cast my foe off. I was in the arms
Of the strong spider. As we went, I grew
Glad, for I thought that now I should be brought
To the great spider's web, and there, mayhap,
Learn the sad fate of her I loved so well.
Up a stark cliff we went, then crossed the web
Just as the red moon bloomed upon the hills
And silvered all the Panticapean vale.
The funnel of the web was in the mouth
Of a vast tomb, whose outside, hewn on rock,
Outlined a Gorgon's face with jaws agape —
Some stern Medusa, Stheno, or Euryale,
Changed to the stone that in the elder days

She changed the sons of men who looked on her.
We passed the funnel, entering the tomb.
About my arms the spider threw his cords,
And shackled them. I dared not move, but lay
Upon the smooth stone floor, inured to fear.
I fancied now that I was safe till dawn.
If I could use my hands I then might find
Some weapon of defense, some club, or stone,
And so resist with some small chance for life.
The thought bred strength. I slowly drew my arms
Upon my sides, and, with persistence, gained
Their freedom; though about the wrists, the flesh
Was bruised and harrowed, and my blood made wet
The spider's cord wherewith I had been bound.

The night seemed endless. As it came to dawn,
A faint moan woke an echo in the tomb.
The echo seemed a cry of pity, sent
For solace to the moan. As light grew strong,
I saw, not far from where I had been laid,
A maiden sitting. All her hair set free,
She made of it a pillow as she leaned
Against the painted wall. My heart threw wide
To her my arms, his hospitable doors;
The guest within, at once the doors were shut.

The sun came up, and spread a cloth of gold
Over the sea. We saw the vale beneath,
And there the town, and fancied where, among
The trees upon the shore, her cottage stood;
Then hoped 'gainst hope to enter it again.

Two thousand years ago, this distant sea
Teemed with the thrifty commerce of the world.
When Athens was, and when her scholars cut,
With thoughts of iron, their own deathless names
Into the stone page of fame, this valé beneath
Held a great city. These, its tombs, endure.
There is no better scoff at the parade
And vanity of life, than that a tomb suggests.

While we looked forth on the historic view,
We saw the subtle spider throw his cord
Over an eagle tangled in the web.
The eagle fought, not mildly overcome,
And spread his wings, and darted his sharp beak.
At last the spider caught him by the neck,
With his serrated claws that grew like horns,
And killed him; then plucked the vanquished plumes,
And sucked the warm blood from the sundered ends.
From this we knew the monster brought us here
To serve a hideous banquet, and that one
Must need be near, and see the other slain.

The web was like the sail of some large ship,
And reached forth from the Gorgon's open mouth,
On either side, to boughs of blighted trees.
Birds were caught in it, and about the place
Wherein the spider hid to watch for prey,
Their bones lay bleaching in the sun and rain.
Upon the web the winds laid violent hands,
And tugged at it, but lacked the sinewed strength

To tear it or divorce it from its place.
The rain left on it when the sun came up,
Dyed the vast cloth with all prismatic hues,
And made it glitter like the silken sail
Of Cleopatra's barge.

We felt quite sure
The eagle's death bequeathed new lease of life.
We cast about at once, in hope to find
Some object for defense. The tomb was strange.
Alone the spider could have known of it.
A rich sarcophagus stood in the midst,
Of deftly inlaid woods, or carved, or bronzed.
Within, a skeleton, its white skull crowned
With gold bestarred with diamonds, chilled my blood.
A bronze lamp, cast to represent the beast
Slain by Bellerophon, the Chimæra,
Was on the floor; and from its lion's mouth
The flame had issued, like the flame of life
That flickered and went out with him gold-crowned.
A target stood near by, and on it clashed
Griffon and stag, adverse as right and wrong.
About, lay cups of onyx set in gold.
On conic jars were bacchanalian scenes, —
Nude chubby Bacchi, grotesque leering fauns,
All linked 'neath vines that grew important grapes;
And in the jars were rings and flowers of gold.
We found twin ear-drops cut from choicest stone,
Metallic mirrors, and a statuette
Of amorous Dido naked to the waist.

Life is a harp, and all its nervous strings,
Touched by the fingers of the fear of death,
Jar with pathetic music. Having found
No trusty implement to bar the way
Of threatening peril, we embraced,
And kissed with silent kisses mixed with tears,
And waited for the end.

When no more,
Hope, like an eagle in the mountain air,
Soars in time's future, it mounts up with wings
Toward the unmapped city walled by death.
Thither the eagle of our hope took flight.

The sun was in the zenith. His back
Toward us, crouched the spider, at the mouth
Of our strange prison on the towering cliff.
The spider's shape was full a fathom long.
Two parts it had, the fore part, head and breast;
The hinder part, the trunk. The first was black,
But all the last was covered with short hair,
Yellow and fine. Eight sprawling legs adhered
To his tough breast. Eight eyes were in his head,
Two in the front, and three on either side;
They had no eyelids, and were never closed,
Protected by a strong transparent nail.
His pincers grew between his foremost eyes —
Were toothed like saws, were venomous, and sharp,
With claws on either end. Two arms stretched out
From his mailed shoulders, and with these he caught

His tangled prey, or guided what he spun.
Slowly the monster turned, and glared at us,
Working his arms, and opening his claws,
Then moved toward us fiercely for attack.
We ran to gain the limit of the tomb
Where darkness was; there as we crouched with dread,
My foot struck some hard substance. In despair
I grasped at it, and with great joy upheld
An ancient sword! — surely, a sharp, bold tooth
To bite the spider. I would sink it deep,
Up to the gum of the crossed guard. Alert,
I sprang upon the monster as he came,
And with one blow cut off his brutish head.
He writhed awhile with pain, but in the end,
Drew up the eight long legs and two thick arms,
And rolling over on his useless back,
Died with a pang.

So we issued forth,
And the green earth seemed happy to be free,
And glad the sky cloud-frescoed 'gainst the blue.
We sought the sea-side cottage, where the chief
Clasped once again his daughter to his breast.
Down from the hill we fetched the spider slain,
And I to science gave these simple facts:
Spiders have no antennæ, therefore rank
Not with the insects. As they breathe with gills
Beneath the body, they possess a heart.

The treasure of the tomb brought wealth to us,
And we who loved were wed one golden day;
And the great Czar hearing our story told,
Sent presents to the bride of silk and pearls.

GRACE BERNARD.

I KNOW the drift and purpose of the years;
The will, which is the magnet of the soul,
Shall yet attain new powers, and man
Be something more than man. The husks fall off;
Old civilizations pass, the new come on.

I.

There are two farms which, smiling in the sun,
Adjoin each other, as I trust, some day
Two hearts will join, who from their bounty live.
One farm is John Bernard's, and one is mine;
And she, the one pearl woman in my eyes,
Is his sweet daughter, gentle Grace Bernard.

Three years ago, my father followed her
Who gave me birth home to his narrow house.
I was at college when death's summons came,
And all the grief fell on me, crushing me;
And all my heart cried out in bitterness,
Moaning to cease with its wet language, — tears.
Then with my prospects of professional life
Thwarted and void, I came back to the farm —

I came back to the love of Grace Bernard.
She was the dove that on the flood of grief
Brought to my window there love's olive spray.
From college to the farm-house where I dwelt
I took my books, friends who are never cold,
With fragile instruments of chemistry,
And cabinets of mineral and rock
With limestone encrinites; asterias
Old as the mountains, or the sea's white lash
Wherewith he smites the shoulders of the shore;
Tarentula and scarabee I brought,
And, too, I brought my diamond microscope
Which magnifies a pin's head to a man's,
And gives me sights in water and in air
The naturalists have not yet touched upon.
Over my fields I wander frequently,
Breaking the past's upturned face of shelving rocks
For special specimens to fill my home;
But find my footsteps always thither tend,
Toward the farm-house of the other farm,
Where Grace Bernard is noontime and delight.

When first I took the hand of her I love,
And held it only as a stranger might,
Some unseen mentor whispered in my ear,
You twain are strands which Destiny shall braid,
And then a numb misgiving, not explained,
Settled with chilly dampness on my heart.
My Grace Bernard in Grace was not misnamed,
There was a soft Madonna look about her eyes;

The long thick lash, the drooping-petal lid,
Wrought on her face all love and tenderness.
Her lips were of that deep intensest red
The cherry, red rose, and columbine wear.
Her golden hair was sunshine changed to silk,
Which fell below her waist, and was a thing
Perhaps some lover, braver far than I,
Might dare to mesh his hands in, or to kiss.

II.

The Spring has come and brought her affluent days,
But in the air a rumor runs of death —
A pestilence is half across the sea.
The presses blare its probable approach,
And poverty and wealth alike forebode.
The cholera it is whispered, Asia-born,
May leave more vacant chairs about our hearths
Than the red havoc of internal war.
There is no foot it may not overtake;
There is no cheek which may not blanch for it.
It is Filth's daughter, and where the low
Huddle in impure air in narrow rooms,
There it must come. As all forms of life,
Animate and inanimate, originate
In seeds and eggs, so all infection does.
The floating gases in the atmosphere
Acting on particles which from filth arise,
Mingle with foul wedlock — germinate,
And bear their seed like grain, or breed like flies.

This product, scattered on the spotless air,
And hurried on the currents of the wind,
Is breathed by human beings, near and far;
And planted in the system, the disease
Ripens and grows, until the sufferer dies.
Yellow fever is vegetable disease
Because the sharp frost kills it. Cholera
Is animal in origin, and survives
The utmost cold of long, dark winter days.

I pray that if the cholera must come,
It will not touch my Grace who is so dear;
But that we twain may at the altar stand,
And outlive many a trouble in the air,
And gather many a day of happiness and peace.

III.

Down by the brook which separates the farms,
Is a great rock that leans above the stream,
And seems some monster of the Saurian day,
That coming to the water's edge to drink,
Was petrified, and so is leaning still.
Upon its back a week ago I sat,
And dreamed of Grace Bernard, and watched the
brook;
And while I dreamed there came within the dream
A premonition of what yet would be.
The future's face, forever turned away,
Now seemed reverted, and its backward look
Was bent on me.

They took a faulty cast
Of Shakespeare's features after he was dead.
I, seeing the future's face, make here my cast.

And this the premonition that was mine —
A perfect premonition full and clear —
And as I know the persons it concerns,
I cannot think it all improbable,
So write it down, that when the time has passed,
I may compare the facts with what is here.
And yet I scarcely should have written this,
Had I not seen his haunting face to-day —
That face which I had never seen before,
Except in my one dream upon the rock
That leans, athirst, above the brimming stream.

The soldier, when he goes to meet the foe,
May darkly understand that death is near,
Yet bravely marches on to destiny.
I too behold a shadow in my path;
I too go on, nor waver in my way.

THE PREMONITION.

I.

Far off, across the turbulence of waves,
I seem to see a wife upon her knees,
Her supplicating hands outstretched to one
Who strikes her with coarse blows on cheek and breast.

He is her husband, and he leaves her there,
And takes her jewels and her only purse,
And in a ship embarks for other shores.
His is the face that I have seen to-day —
A handsome face whatever be its sins:
A firm mouth, with large wandering black eyes,
A bearded under-lip, and snowy teeth;
Long, fine black hair, which idly falls about
Shoulders that stoop from labor over books;
Withal a high and intellectual brow,
Not broad enough to hold a generous soul.

II.

I see the farm-house where my Grace abides;
The afternoon is clear, the grass is green;
And Grace comes forth and walks toward the brook.
Beside its bank, which is a slope of moss,
I see the face intent upon the scene.
Now Grace draws near, and starting back to find
A stranger in the dell she loves the most,
Is half attracted by his cultured mien,
And half repelled by inconsistent fears.
He rises, bowing low, and begs to speak:
He has not seen such beauty in his life;
He craves to touch a finger of her hand,
To judge if she be of the earth, or one
Upon some holy mission from that land
Whereto, with fastings and with many prayers,
Through God's good grace he hopes yet to attain.

Then John Bernard, who has been working near,
Seeding the furrows for his empty barns,
This stranger and my Grace puts hand in hand.
I see her smile in answer to his smiles.
She makes her ears his cells for honeyed speech;
And yet she seems to fear him for some cause.
Now, as the slow sun tarries on the hills,
I see them parting at the farm-house door —
The wide half-door which now is opened half —
And as he passes down the bordered path,
His kiss still lingering upon her hand,
She leans out from the door, and watches him
Until he vanishes between the trees.
I seem to see her face, a trouble sweet
Dwelling upon it, even though the light
Sets it in glory, with a slender ring
Above the white brow and the golden hair.

III.

I see them riding down the village street:
He on a horse as black and strong as iron,
She on her snowy palfrey, robed in green,
Slack reins in hand; the horses side by side.
Even as I see and write, my heart grows cold —
Cold as a bird that on a winter's day
Breasts the bleak wind, high in the biting air.

IV.

I see a city with a concourse vast
Of gas-lit streets and buildings, and above,
Its dear face buried in its cloudy hands,
The Night bends over, weeping. In the street
I see the face again I saw to-day.

I see him writing in a narrow room.
I read the words:
To-night I end my life.
The river says "Embrace, I offer rest."
The world and I have grappled in fair fight,
And I am beaten. Having found defeat,
I long to go down to its lowest depths.
I only ask, that those who find these words,
Will send them to my people past the sea;
To-night I cross a wider: so, adieu.
MICHAEL GIANNI.

This is his true name,
And afterward he writes his wife's address.
He leaves the paper foldless on a stand,
And then goes forth; but not to end his life.
He dreams that now his life is but begun.
He sees my Grace in all his coming days;
He sees the large old farm-house where she dwells,
And therein hopes to happily pass the years,
Living in peace and plenty till he dies.

Most human calculations end in loss,
And every one who has a plan devised,
Is like a foolish walker on a rope,
First balancing on this side, then on that,
Hazarding much to gain a paltry end;
And if the rope of calculation breaks,
Or if the foot slip, added to mishap
Come the world's jeers and gibes; and so 'tis best.
Should half men's schemings find success at last,
I fear God's plans would have but narrow room.

(Michael Gianni, now I know your name,
This premonition gives the hint to me
To trip you in your studied subtleties.
You will not win my Grace, who loves me still;
You will not dare to kiss her hand again.)

V.

Beneath a rustic arbor, near her house,
Linked with sweet converse, sit two shadowed forms.
The new sword moon against the violet sky
Is held aloft, by one white arm of cloud
Raised from the sombre shoulder of a hill.
My Grace and I are sitting in the bower,
And down upon my breast and girdling arm
Is strewn pure gold — no alloy mixes it —
The pure ore of her lovable gold hair.
The cunning weavers of Arabia,
Who seek to shuttle sunshine in their silk,

Would give its weight in diamonds for this hair,
Whereof to make a fabric for their king.

I see the trees that skirt the yonder vale,
And where the road dents down between their arms,
I see a figure passing to and fro.
Now he comes near, and striding up the path
Enters the arbor, and discovers us.
It is Gianni; to his flashing eyes
A fierce deep hatred leaps up from his heart,
As lightning, which forebodes the nearing storm,
Leaps luridly above the midnight hills.
With some excuse Gianni passes on,
While Grace, with sweetly growing confidence,
Whispers with lips which slightly touch my ear,
"I never loved him, I was always yours."

VI.

I see the parlor that my Grace adorns
With flowers and with her presence, which is far
Above the fragrant presence of all flowers.
Grace sits at her piano; on her lips
A song of twilight and the evening star.
There as the shadows slowly gather round,
Gianni comes, and stops a moody hour;
She, ice to his approaches; he, despair;
But ere he goes, he places in her hand
A large ripe orange, fresh from Sicily,
And begs her to accept it for his sake.

She bows him from the room, and puts the fruit
Before her on her music, once again
Dreaming of me, and singing some wild song
Of Pan, who, by the river straying down,
Cut reeds, and blew upon them with such power,
He charmed the lilies and the dragon-flies.
Now while the song is swaying to its close,
I seem to come myself into the room,
And clasp true arms about my darling Grace;
She lays Gianni's orange in my hand,
And says that I must eat it; she would not
Have taken it, but that she did not wish
To cross him with refusal. So I say,
"Surely this stranger has peculiar taste
To bring an orange to you — only one.
Perhaps there is more in it than we know."

VII.

I seem to have this orange in my room,
And in the light of morning turn it round.
I find no flaw in it on any side.
A goodly orange, ripe, with tender coat
Of that deep reddish yellow, like fine gold.
Perhaps the tree had wrapped its roots about
A chest of treasure, and had drawn the wealth
Into its heart to spend it on its fruit.
But while I slowly turn the orange round,
And look more closely, lo, the slightest cut! —
A deep incision made by some sharp steel.

I carefully cut the rind, and without once
Breaking the fine apartments of the fruit,
Or spilling thence a drop of golden juice,
Find that one room through which the steel has passed.
This I dissect, and, testing as I can,
Fail to discover aught that's poisonous.

VIII.

I bring my microscope, and on a seed
Clinging with abject fear, I see a Shape
Whose wings are reeking with foul slime, whose eyes
Glare with a demon lustre born of Pain.
Its face has somewhat of the human shape,
The under-jaw too large, and bearded long;
The forehead full of putrefying sores.
Such front the Genius, Danhasch, may have worn.
It may be that the hideous face is like
The idol Krishna's, from whose feasts depart,
Smitten with cholera, the Hindoo devotees.
The body oozes with a loathsome dew.
Its head is red as if sucked full of blood;
But all the rest, its hundred legs, and tail,
The mailed back, and the wide-webbed prickly wings,
Are green, like those base eyes of jealousy
Which hope to see a covert murder done.

I find the finest needle in the house,
And press the point down on the slimy hide.
The blunt edge crushes, does not pierce the shape,
And brings the struggle that I gloat to see.
The legs stretch out, and work to get away;
A barbed tongue and twin fangs drool from the mouth.
The eyes protrude, and glare with deadly hate,
Until they fix at last in stony calm.

I ponder long on what this shape can be.
There is no doubt Gianni placed it here;
If so, where has he caught and caged a thing
The naked eye has not the power to see?
Its uses must be deadly. In revenge,
He hopes to take the life of her I love.
While poisons of another character
Might be detected, this remains unknown.
The Thing I have discovered — this vile Shape,
Must be an atom of some foul disease!
And now I have the secret. For some days
Gianni waits upon a stricken man,
Who dies, a victim of the cholera.
In some strange manner he has found this germ,
And placed it in the orange, hoping thus
To bring the dread disease to Grace Bernard.

IX.

I seem to be with him I hate, once more,
And now accuse him of the fiendish deed

That I through chance averted. Now I too
Command him to return to his true wife,
And no more cross my path; should he remain,
He shall but wait to meet her, for my words
Already have been sent that he is here.

X.

I know that I shall fall sick dangerously,
And in some way by dark Gianni's hand.
I seem to lie asleep upon my bed,
And Grace is near, and watching my calm face.
The village doctor makes his morning call,
And takes my listless hand to feel the pulse.
There is no pulse! His hand goes to the heart.
My heart has ceased to beat, and all is still.
The hand the doctor held drops down like lead.
A looking-glass receives no fading mist,
Laid on the icy and immovable lips.
My eyes are fixed; I glare upon them all.
Grace twines her widowed arms about my neck,
Kissing my sallow cheeks, with hopeless tears,
Calling my name, and begging me come back;
So, thinking me dead, they close my staring eyes,
And put the face-cloth over my white face,
And go with silent tread about the room.
They do not know that I am in a trance.
I hear each whisper uttered, and the sighs
That heave the desolate bosom of my Grace.

XI.

All is so dark since they have shut my eyes;
I think it cruel in them to do that—
Shut out the light of day and every chance
That I could ever have of seeing Grace.
I cannot move a muscle, and I try,
And strive to part my lips to say some word;
But all in vain; the mind has lost control
Over the body's null machinery.

I wonder if they yet will bury me,
Thinking me dead? To wake up in the grave,
And hear a wagon rumbling overhead,
Or a chance footstep passing near the spot,
And then cry out and never get reply;
But hear the footstep vanish far away,
And know the cold mould smothers up all cries,
And is above, beneath, and round me,
Is bitter thought. To lie back then and die,
Suffocating slowly while I tear my hair,
Makes me most wild to think of.

XII.

Hark! 'tis night.
The hour is borne distinctly by the wind.
My Grace sits near me; now comes to my side,
And unto Him, whose ear is everywhere,
She, kneeling down, puts up her hands, and prays.

"O Father of all mercies, still be merciful,
And raise me from the gulf of this despair.
I cannot think nor feel my love is dead.
If he yet lives, and lingers in a trance,
Give me some sign that I may know the truth."

I slowly raise my hand, and let it fall.

Grace springs up all delight, and draws the cloth,
Kissing my lips, and begging me to wake.
I try, but fail to raise my hand again.
The trance still lasts. My eyes will not unclose;
My lips refuse the functions of their place.

XIII.

On the next day will be the funeral;
But Grace has this delayed for one week more;
Yet all in vain, I neither wake nor move.

I hear the people coming in the house,
And straight within my coffin long to rise.
I hear the pastor's prayer, and then his words,
Simple and good, and full of tender praise.
They come at last to take a parting look,
A file of faces that pass out the door.
I hear them quickly screwing down the lid;
And now the bearers take me from the house,
And push me, feet first, in the black plumed hearse.
Gianni is a bearer of my pall,

And Grace is choked with sobs, and follows on.
We reach the grave. They slowly lower me down.
Some gravel on the side is loose, and falls
Rattling upon the narrow coffin lid.

Horror on horror! Let me see no more!

AFTER BURIAL.

So stands the premonition; and to-day
I look back on the words here written down,
Comparing them with what has happened since,
And find there is no flaw in any scene.

Always intending to tell Grace my fear
That some day I might be entombed alive,
I always failed, until it was too late.
But as the sod fell on the coffin-lid,
My trance was broken, and I called and screamed,
Until they drew me up from out the grave,
And breaking in my prison, set me free.

Gianni fled, fearing my face at last.
To-day I have his letter from his home,
Beneath the far-off skies of Italy,
Craving forgiveness for his wrongs to me;
Saying that he repents for all his past,
And with Christ's help, will lead a better life.
He found his wife and children overjoyed
To have him back again to their embrace.

To-morrow Grace Bernard and I shall wed.
The bell that tolled my bitter funeral knell,
Will ring, glad of my wedding and my bride —
Ring merrily round and round a jubilant peal.

There comes no premonition now to show to me
What the long future has in store for us;
But from my door I watch the sunset skies,
And see blue mountains tower o'er golden plains,
Clothed with pure beauty stretching far away.
So seems the future. I await the morn.

VEERA.

I.

THE KING'S SEAL.

WHILE yet upon his couch our father lay,
Sick unto death, my brothers, with one mind,
Plotted abrupt destruction to my life.
I did not tell the king, because I feared
To lessen by one beat the throbbing of his heart.
Beside his couch I knelt, and bowed my head —
I, his first-born, whom all the people loved.
His hot, weak hand he laid upon my hair,
And blessed me with his blessing, then said on:
"Thou hast beheld in Spring the dark green blade
That stabs up through the unresisting earth;
At last the Summer crowns it with a flower.
So thou, when I am passed away, and gone to dust,
Shalt wear a crown, but grander than the shrubs —
The symbol of a kingdom, on thy brow.
But take thee now this lesson to thy heart,
And from the grass learn wisdom; wear thy crown
As meekly, and as void of all display,
As doth the shrub half hidden under leaves."

So he bent down with pain, and kissed my cheek,
As though, having issued a great law, he
Had set his seal upon it — the king's seal.

I cared not for the crown, save as a means
To give my soul a higher and a nobler life.
This my old tutor taught me — a strange man he,
With careless garb, and heavy hairy brows
Bridged over eyes that shone like furnace fire.
My will was lost in his. I grew like him.
I only cared to study and to dream.
And he it was who, standing in the night
Between two pillars on the palace porch,
Saw my two brothers pass, and overheard
The hateful whisper of their black design.

II.

THE NIGHT OF THE ESCAPE.

The night before the murder was to be,
I drew my long, keen dagger from its sheath,
And stole on down the marble stair-way, past
The throne-room, to the curtained arch wherein
My brothers lay asleep. No dream beset
The guilty Dead-Sea of their rest. They lay
Engulfed in pillows, like two ships mid waves.
I saw their faces, and the one was fair.
Long dark brown hair fell from his noble brow,
And on the silken billow of the couch lay curled
Like spray. The other face was cold and dark

I felt no pity in my angry breast
For this, the older brother of the twain.
Yet he it was who always praised me most.
Praise is a dust of diamond that, if thrown
Well in the eyes of even noble men,
Will blind them to a host of flagrant faults.
The moon was full, and 'twixt two silvered clouds
Looked forth, like any princess from between
The tasseled curtains of her downy bed.
The vagrant wind came through the opened blind,
And whispered of the desert; with its hand
Fanning the flame that in the silver urn
Mimicked a star. Beneath the rays I wrote:
I should have slain you both for your intent
Of murder; but I spare you, and I go.
So, take the kingdom, and rule long and well.
Between them there I laid the paper down,
Then thrust my dagger, to the golden hilt,
Through it, deep in the couch. So passing on,
I came to that high room wherein my sire,
The king, lay sick, and drifting near to death.
My tutor at his feet, and on the floor,
Embraced by needed sleep, lay like a dog.
I came to see the king's face once again,
Ere, like a maid who in her lover trusts,
I gave myself up, body and soul,
To the great desert and the world beyond.
How sweetly slept the king! His long white beard,
And venerable face, were undisturbed
By even the breezy motion of his breath.

Surely, I thought, the fever must have passed.
I bent down tenderly to kiss the cheek.
How cold! God help me, can the king be dead?
My heart gave one wild bound, driving a wave
Of grief, vast as a mountain, up the sands
Of my bleak desolation. The wave broke
Into a blinding mist of tears at last.
I longed to moan out my despair, but paused,
Checking my sobs to kiss the face once more;
Then moved from the strange room, parting with care
The massive silken curtains, fearful then
Their rustle might attract some wakeful ear.
I found the jewels of the crown, and these
With all my own I in a bag secured,
And hung about my neck, beneath my robe.
Noiseless as a ghost I passed the hall,
And down the stair-way wrought of sandal-wood
Made lightest footsteps. As I stole
Along the alcoves where the maidens slept,
A lady stood before me. She outstretched
Her white and naked arms, and round my neck
Entwined them. She was the captive, Veera,
Once held for ransom from some Bedouin tribe;
But when the coin was brought she would not go;
At this the king was pleased, for thus she made
Perpetual peace between him and her kin.
No maid in Mesched up and down, was found
To rival her for beauty. All her words
Were apt and good, and all her ways were sweet.
I, in her happy prison, ivory-barred

By her white arms, was restless for release.
She would not set me free until I told
The purport of my vigil, and revealed
The place whereat my journey would be done.
I did not wait to pay her back her kiss.
I hurried to the stables, where I found
My coal-black steed. He neighed and pawed the floor.
I bound the saddle firmly, grasped the reins,
And in a moment passed the city's gate,
And shot out on the desert, where the wind
Made race with us, but lagged behind at last.

III.

TWO PROBLEMS.

Vienna gained, I gave myself to books.
Here I had promised Veera I should be.
New paths were opened to me, and my days
Were lost in study. All my tutor knew
Seemed cramped and meagre in these wider ways
Of thought and science. Better far, I said,
To know, than be a king. There is no crown
That so becomes the brow as knowledge does.

To solve two problems, now engrossed my life.
My Bedouin tutor had spent all his days
Upon them, but without success. On me
He grafted all the purpose of his soul,
Determined, though he failed, that I might yet
Toil on when he was compassed round by death.

These sister problems were, *How make pure gold?*
And, *How endure forever on the earth?*

IV.

THE DOOR.

Among the books that I had bought myself,
I found the Bible. This to peruse
I soon essayed; but ere I had read far,
Behold! I found the door behind which lay
The answers to my problems. Locked and barred
The door was, yet I knew it was the door.
For here I read of Eden, and that in the midst
The Tree of Life stood, while through the land
A river ran which parted in four heads;
And one was Gihon, the Ethiop stream;
And one was Pison, the great crystal tide
Which floods Havilah, where fine gold is found,
And rare bdellium and the onyx stone.
So, as my tutor said, my problems were
A dual secret, and the one contained
The other. All the long night through I pored
Above the words, and kissed the unconscious page
With reverent lips. My heart was like a sponge
Soaked in the water of the mystic words.

V.

THE KEY.

As one who in the night, passing a street
Deserted, finds a lost key rusted and old,

Yet knows that it will fit some great iron door
Behind which countless treasures are concealed,
So I, when first I came to Mesmer's works,
Knew I had found the key to move the door
Of my twin problems. Then, day after day,
I made them all my study. Much I mourned
The sad disheartened life that Mesmer led.
He never knew that one good thing, success;
But yet his strong, persistent genius, to the end
Endured. Yet such the rule in every age.
The one true man appears, and gives his thought,
At which the whole world rail or basely sneer.
The next man comes and makes a thankless use
Of what the other knew, and wins the praise
The first man lost by being ripe too soon.

VI.

NEWS FROM MESCHED.

Down the long street, upon my iron-black steed,
I rode and pondered. Where shall I seek to find
A sweet soul pure as dawn, who to my will shall be
Both malleable and ductile; who can soar
Over the whole earth, or go back in the past?
While yet I mused, lo, up a garden walk,
A lady chased a bird. An empty cage
Stood in the vine-clad cottage-window near.
The bird was like some sweet elusive thought;
The maid, a Sappho, weary with pursuit.
She only glanced my way to see me pass,

Then turned and ran towards me, her large eyes
With gladness scintillant. It was the maid,
Veera. Her hand upon my shoulder, up the walk
We went, my steed following, while her bird,
Tired of his liberty, had found his cage.
Strange news had Veera. Here she lived in peace;
But through the city she had sought me long.
When I was gone from Mesched, and my brothers read
The paper I had written, their wrath rose
Against my tutor whom they deemed the spy.
He, being found asleep beside the king
Who lay dead, to his door they brought
The baseless charge of murder. Through the streets
They sent their criers to proclaim the deed.
So, clamorous for his life, the people came
And dragged him forth, and led him to the block
And slew him. On a spear they set his head,
And placed it high upon the tower above
The eastern gate. The birds pecked at the eyes,
And of the hair made comfortable nests.
The rain beat on it, and the active wind
Crowned it with desert dust. Always the sun
Made salutation to it, flushing it
Until it seemed more ghastly than before.
But after this mad crime the older brother grew
Jealous of him, the younger. One dark morn
They found the last-born lifeless in the street,
Stabbed by a long, sharp poniard in the back.
Misrule followed misrule, and justice fled.

Laws were abolished, and pleasure's lewdest voice
Hawked in the market-place, and through the streets.
Her story done, Veera entreated me
To set my face for Mesched with the dawn.
"Not yet," I said, "not yet." And then I made
Strange passes with my hands, and braced my will,
To sway her will; then with a questioning glance
She passed out to a calm Mesmeric sleep.
So, well I knew that I had found the soul
My purpose needed, and I bade her wake.

VII.

THE MIDNIGHT VISITOR.

I sat and pondered in my room that night
Until the towers and steeples, near and far,
Like sentries of the sky, issued the hour
Of midnight. Then I wrought magnetic force
With waving hands; and set my swerveless will
That Veera should approach me, and that none
Should harm or see her as she passed the streets.
At last I heard her footstep on the stair —
The patter of her feet as soft as rain,
And then she turned the hinge and entered in.
A long white wrapper made of satin, bound
With lace of gold, and fastened at the throat
With buttons of cut diamond, clad her form.
A band of opals was around her neck —
A hundred little worlds with central fires.
Her feet were naked, and her hair was down.

Her large eyes, wide and staring, took no heed
Of anything before them; thus she slept.
I bade her sit beside me, and I placed
The Bible on her knee, and laid her hand
Upon the verse that names the tree of life.
"Tell me," I said, "where may this tree be found."
"The way is long," she answered me at last,
"And I am worn and weary. I have tracked
The shore of one long river, many a mile.
The sun scorches like fire. I am athirst.
I cannot find the tree; my search is done."
"Look down the past, and find if any knew
Where grows this tree, or how it might be found."
Again her lips made answer: "One I see,
Long dead, who bends above a written scroll,
And therein makes strange characters, which hold
Some hidden sense pertaining to this tree.
In Milan, in the Ambrosian library there,
I see this scroll to-night; 'tis worn with age."

"Now seek thy home again," I said, "sweet soul.
Thou art as meek and pure as him whose hand
First wrote God's words." So she arose, and passed
Along the dark, deserted street, and I
Followed her closely, till I saw her cross
The threshold of her cottage; then I turned,
And found my home, and calmly slept till dawn.

VIII.

THE PALIMPSEST.

In Milan, in the Ambrosian library there,
Among Pinellian writings seared with age,
I found a prophet's palimpsest — a scroll
That Angelo Maio had brought to light.
And on the margin of this scroll, I found
Mysterious signs which baffled me at first.
After a full week's search I chanced to find
The mongrel dialect of which they were.
I thus translated: *Gihon is the Nile.*
A perfect soul may find long life and gold.
Surely, I thought, Veera the maid is pure.
Her life's blue sky has not one cloud of sin.
If her feet press the soil where Eve first trod,
I can but follow and attain. So I
Back to Vienna came and found Veera.
To her I made my double purpose plain,
And prayed her to go with me in my search.
She smiled assent. To be near me, she said,
Had brought her to Vienna; this indeed
Detained her from her kinsmen. Her heart's book
Lay open to me, and I read her love.
So we were wed, and both lives ran to one.

IX.

GIHON.

Now for the Nile we journeyed, gaining first
The town of Gondokoro, where the stream
Of Bahr el Abiad, or White Nile, flows.
Thence we passed on, and with the savage kings
Of Karagwe, Uganda and Ungoro, stopped,
To rest our weary feet, or in their huts
Escape the sun's fierce glare. At last we found
The sources of the Nile; two lakes that now
Are called Nyanza and Nzige. If here
I had but paused, and had retraced my steps,
The whole world would have known and praised my name,
For I was first to find the secret out.
But then I cared not for it, journeying on.
After a week, we came upon a land
All void, and barren of a single leaf.
Veera was pale and worn, although she bore
Fatigue with generous patience for my sake.
Our feet were swollen, and with the hot sand scorched,
Our garments were in tatters, and we seemed
Like beggars, in a land where there were none to give.
At night we slept beside a wide, cool stream,
Whereat we quenched our thirst, and bathed our feet.
My beard was grown, and all my hair hung down

Neglected, on my shoulders. I was weak,
And thin, and feverish, and Veera, too,
I saw was sick, and languished hour by hour.

X.

GOLD!

In the sand, lo! something to the sun
Replied with brilliant lustre; as I brushed
The dust away, I saw that it was gold! —
A solid bar of gold — and yet so weak
Was I, I could not move it from its place.
I would have given then the bar of gold
To buy a crust, but could not. So we passed,
And came where five great rivers went their ways.
Which should we follow? One I knew
Led to the tree of life, but all the rest
Went back to death. Here a dead bird we found,
And tearing off its gaudy plumage, ate.
Upon occasional trees grew strange sparse fruits,
And these sustained us as we wandered on.
Along the banks for many a mile we went
By each of these five rivers, then returned.
So all my hope was dead, and long I prayed
That I might live to see my land again.

XI.

THE MESSAGE OF THE THREE MEN.

The night came on, and unto sleep we gave
Our spirits. When the golden day was born

Veera awoke, and told me all her dream;
"Lo, in the night three men have talked with me—
Three strange good men who said the kindest words,
And said that only those who were released
From sin, could find the garden of the Lord.
And this release was bought upon a cross
By One, a Nazarene, with priceless blood.
If He would bear our sins, then we might reach
The garden; but we must not touch or eat
The tree of life that flourished in the midst."
Then I abased my soul, and prayed again,
And cast off all the burden of my sins,
Tearing my strange ambition from my heart.
And Veera, too, embraced the Christian Faith.
So we arose, and went upon our way,
And journeying eastward, Eden found at last!

XII.

THE GARDEN.

The trees were housed with nests, and every one
Was like a city of song. The streams too
Were voluble; they laughed and gurgled there
Like men who, at a banquet, sit and drink
And chatter. All the grass was like a robe
Of velvet, and there was no need of rain.
In dells roofed with green leafage, nature spread
Couches meet for a Sybarite. Sweet food
The servant trees extended us to eat
In their long, branchy arms. Even the sun

Was tempered, and the sky was always blue.
Corpulent grapes along the crystal rocks,
Made consorts of the long-robed lady leaves.
The butterfly and bee, from morn till eve,
Consulted with the roses, lip to lip,
Which grew in rank profusion. They at times
Dared to invade the empire of the grass,
And overthrew its green-robed, spear-armed hosts.
The lilies too were like an army there,
And every night they struck their snowy tents,
To please their great commander, the round moon —
God's lily in the everlasting sky.

XIII.

CAST OUT.

As to the heliotrope comes fluttering down
The peacock-butterfly, who sips and flies,
So each glad day gold-winged came to the land
And sipped its sip of time and fled away.
Now in an evil hour I hungered, and I saw
The tree of life that grew forbidden fruit.
What harm, I thought, is there to always live?
To live is happiness; but to die is pain.
The rental claimed by death falls due too soon.
So I reached forth, and took the fruit, and ate.
Then all the sky grew dark, and from the land
Malignant terrors drove me shrieking forth;
And as I fled, my youth abandoned me;
My hair turned gray, my shoulders stooped, my blood

Grew colder, and my perfect form was changed.
A weak old man with wrinkled face, I fled,
To wander in the wastes. Once I looked back
Upon the garden; over it the sky
Was soft and clear; and midway in the air
I saw Veera between two angels, borne
To heaven. So I turned again and fled.

XIV.

"LONG LIVE THE KING."

I came at last to Mesched. It was night.
The moon, half-shadowed, trailed its silver robe
Over the tower above the eastern gate,
And there revealed the outlines of a skull
Set on a spear. The portals were unbarred.
I passed the arch, but in the shadow kept,
While on the flinty wall I edged my knife.
Then I crept on until I gained the porch
Of the great palace. There I smote the guard,
And entering in, sought out the sleeping king.
Deep in his heart I plunged my thirsty knife.
All the next day I sat before the gate,
And begged, and heard the rumors of the town;
Then, standing forth, I claimed to be their king,
And told them all my story to the end.
None pitied the dead ruler, for he knew
No pity while he lived. So I was king at last;
But all my life, and all my hope to me

Are dust and ashes, knowing that God's frown
Abides upon me. Would that I could die!

There is no kindlier spirit than content.
And there is nothing better in the world
Than to do good, and trust in God for all.

www.ingramcontent.com/pod-product-compliance
Lightning Source LLC
LaVergne TN
LVHW021416110826
845150LV00007B/1946

9781425510022